TO

FROM

DATE

GOD'S GIFT
FOR
FATHERS

JACK
COUNTRYMAN

COUNTRYMAN®
A Division of Thomas Nelson Publishers

THOMAS NELSON
Since 1798

God's Gift for Fathers
© 2017 by Jack Countryman

Published in Nashville, Tennessee, by Thomas Nelson®. Thomas Nelson is a registered trademark of HarperCollins Christian Publishing, Inc.

Scripture quotations are taken from the New King James Version®. © 1982 by Thomas Nelson. Used by permission. All rights reserved.

Cover design by Studio Gearbox
Interior design by Kristy Edwards

ISBN-13: 978-0-7180-8996-2

Printed in China

17 18 19 20 21 TIMS 5 4 3 2 1

Introduction

A father's life is filled with many responsibilities: to provide for his family, to be the spiritual leader, and to give wisdom to his children. This book brings to light the fact that in God's eyes the role of a father is an important part of His creation. God's Word is a beacon of light that will guide your steps through the many challenges you will face. My father was the light that showed me how to live for Christ at an early age. May this book help you be the father God has called you to be.

Contents

God's Wisdom to Bless Your Family . . .

God's Dynamic Example of Fathers

Scripture Meditations for Fathers

Crisis Scripture Guide

GOD FILLS A FATHER WITH JOY WHEN . . .

He Praises the Lord

Psalm 150:6 says, "Let everything that has breath praise the LORD." As long as we have breath, we must acknowledge the power and majesty of our Lord. We are to praise Him when we get up in the morning, praise Him in the car, praise Him at work—wherever we are, we should seek to honor Him. First Thessalonians 5:18 says, "In everything give thanks; for this is the will of God in Christ Jesus for you." You may not understand what is happening in your life, but God's will in every circumstance is that you praise Him and thank Him in all things. When you do this, God will give you a peace that passes all understanding.

Praise the LORD!
Praise God in His sanctuary;
Praise Him in His mighty firmament!
Praise Him for His mighty acts;
Praise Him according to His excellent
   greatness! . . .
Let everything that has breath praise the LORD.
Praise the LORD!

—PSALM 150:1–2, 6

Great is the LORD, and greatly to be praised;
And His greatness is unsearchable.
One generation shall praise Your works to another,
And shall declare Your mighty acts.

—PSALM 145:3–4

Be anxious for nothing, but in everything by prayer
and supplication, with thanksgiving, let your requests
be made known to God; and the peace of God, which
surpasses all understanding, will guard your hearts and
minds through Christ Jesus.

—PHILIPPIANS 4:6–7

His Children Grow to Love the Lord

A father's ability for helping his children grow in the Lord is a reason to shout for joy because he is doing exactly what he has been called by God to do. The very essence of being a father to your children is helping them build a foundation for living a life filled with the Holy Spirit. As you lead your children closer to Him, God will protect and guide your children as they walk through life, and you will experience His peace, knowing that He is with them. Therefore, teach your children daily to honor God and live for Him; it is the only way to be happy in the Lord.

Train up a child in the way he should go,
And when he is old he will not depart from it.
—Proverbs 22:6

Jesus said to him, "'You shall love the Lord your God
with all your heart, with all your soul, and with all
your mind.' This is the first and great commandment.
And the second is like it: 'You shall love your neighbor
as yourself.'"
—Matthew 22:37–39

Christ may dwell in your hearts through faith; that
you, being rooted and grounded in love, may be able
to comprehend with all the saints what is the width
and length and depth and height—to know the love of
Christ which passes knowledge; that you may be filled
with all the fullness of God.
—Ephesians 3:17–19

I love those who love me,
And those who seek me diligently will find me.
—Proverbs 8:17

He Worships the Lord

The Bible speaks often of worship and invites you to come with a pure heart to worship the Lord in the beauty of holiness. There are many reasons the Lord is worthy to be praised: His power, His majesty, His righteousness, and His love among them. And worship, the act of acknowledging God's strength and benevolence, is part of your responsibility and privilege as a Christian. When you honor God with worship and come to Him with an open heart, you will be blessed and filled with His presence. When you begin each day with worship and prayer, you will be reminded to walk closely with Him. Diligently seek to honor Him throughout your day, and you will be blessed.

Give to the LORD the glory due His name;
    Bring an offering, and come before Him.
    Oh, worship the LORD in the beauty of holiness!
                —1 CHRONICLES 16:29

Oh come, let us sing to the LORD!
    Let us shout joyfully to the Rock of our salvation.
    Let us come before His presence with
        thanksgiving;
    Let us shout joyfully to Him with psalms.
    For the LORD is the great God,
    And the great King above all gods.
                —PSALM 95:1–3

Oh come, let us worship and bow down;
    Let us kneel before the LORD our Maker.
    For He is our God,
    And we are the people of His pasture,
    And the sheep of His hand.
                —PSALM 95:6–7

GOD LISTENS TO
A FATHER'S PRAYER
WHEN . . .

Trials Run Rampant

Sometimes in life you seem to meet trouble at every turn. God often uses trials to position you for greater blessings. Even in times of great disappointment, He has your best in mind. He knows how He wants to use disappointments and hardships for your benefit. During these trials, He desires that you see Him as your only source of salvation and blessing. If you are in a physically or emotionally difficult spot right now, refuse to become discouraged. Ask the Lord to reveal His plan for your life. Commit yourself fully to Him, no matter what it costs. God will provide for you in ways that far exceed human understanding.

*For I know the thoughts that I think toward you, says
the LORD, thoughts of peace and not of evil, to give
you a future and a hope. . . . And you will seek Me
and find Me, when you search for Me with all your
heart.*

—JEREMIAH 29:11, 13

*"Ask, and it will be given to you; seek, and you will
find; knock, and it will be opened to you."*

—MATTHEW 7:7

*Give ear to my words, O LORD,
    Consider my meditation.
    Give heed to the voice of my cry,
    My King and my God,
    For to You I will pray.
    My voice You shall hear in the morning, O LORD;
    In the morning I will direct it to You,
    And I will look up.*

—PSALM 5:1–3

He Asks for Patience

As a father, there are many days you need patience with your children, with your spouse, in your work, and with the various circumstances you encounter in life. In James 1:2, you are encouraged to "count it all joy when you fall into various trials." But why? Not because these circumstances are pleasant, but because they are profitable. Trials and tribulations produce patience; in difficulty, you learn to endure, to bear up, to persevere, to keep holding on despite momentary suffering. The patience you develop makes you stronger in your walk with Christ because you are less likely to become entangled in sin. And He will help you as you lean on Him for patience.

My brethren, count it all joy when you fall into various trials, knowing that the testing of your faith produces patience. But let patience have its perfect work, that you may be perfect and complete, lacking nothing.

—JAMES 1:2–4

Therefore we also, since we are surrounded by so great a cloud of witnesses, let us lay aside every weight, and the sin which so easily ensnares us, and let us run with endurance the race that is set before us.

—HEBREWS 12:1

Be kindly affectionate to one another with brotherly love . . . fervent in spirit, serving the Lord; rejoicing in hope, patient in tribulation, continuing steadfastly in prayer.

—ROMANS 12:10–12

He Asks for Guidance

God has given you the Holy Spirit so that He can guide you in every area of your life. With the Spirit's help, you become a better father, husband, and witness for His glory. But in order to receive His blessings of wisdom, you must come to the Lord and be willing to learn from Him. The more you seek His wisdom, the more He generously provides. And when you place your faith in the Lord, He comes into your heart and, through the Spirit, He sets you free from the bondage of sin, the sting of death, and your futile attempts to become righteous by your own efforts. If you ask, God will continue to transform your life.

"And I will pray the Father, and He will give you another Helper, that He may abide with you forever—the Spirit of truth, whom the world cannot receive, because it neither sees Him nor knows Him; but you know Him, for He dwells with you and will be in you."

—JOHN 14:16–17

Where the Spirit of the Lord is, there is liberty. But we all, with unveiled face, beholding as in a mirror the glory of the Lord, are being transformed into the same image from glory to glory, just as by the Spirit of the Lord.

—2 CORINTHIANS 3:17–18

"If anyone thirsts, let him come to Me and drink. He who believes in Me, as the Scripture has said, out of his heart will flow rivers of living water." But this He spoke concerning the Spirit, whom those believing in Him would receive; for the Holy Spirit was not yet given, because Jesus was not yet glorified.

—JOHN 7:37–39

He Confesses Sin and Seeks Forgiveness

Sin blocks your fellowship with the Lord, and it keeps you from experiencing God's goodness. But when you're mired in sin, how do you regain your communion with God? David wrote in Psalm 32:1, "Blessed is he whose transgression is forgiven, whose sin is covered." As long as he had not repented from his sin, David knew that he could not enjoy the fullness of God's presence. The same is true for you if you are carrying a sin that you need to take to the Lord. Turn to God in prayer, asking Him to apply His forgiveness to your life so that you can receive His mercy. He loves you and wants you to enjoy fellowship with Him.

Blessed is he whose transgression is forgiven,
    Whose sin is covered.
    Blessed is the man to whom the Lord does not
        impute iniquity,
    And in whose spirit there is no deceit. . . .
    I acknowledged my sin to You,
    And my iniquity I have not hidden.
    I said, "I will confess my transgressions to the
        Lord,"
    And You forgave the iniquity of my sin. . . .
    You are my hiding place;
    You shall preserve me from trouble;
    You shall surround me with songs of deliverance.
        —Psalm 32:1–2, 5, 7

*He has delivered us from the power of darkness and
conveyed us into the kingdom of the Son of His love,
in whom we have redemption through His blood, the
forgiveness of sins.*

    —Colossians 1:13–14

Responsibilities Overwhelm Him

Could anything feel more discouraging or frightening than facing a terrible trial all by yourself? It can be paralyzing to imagine having no one to lean on during times of crisis. But God assures you that if you know Him, you will never have to worry about facing life alone. He is right there with you, in easy times and in the difficult ones too. You can always count on the Lord, for He has promised never to leave you nor forsake you. Run to Him; tell Him what is on your heart and seek His wisdom. Learn to listen to the Holy Spirit, and He will guide you through every difficult situation you face.

"For the mountains shall depart
And the hills be removed,
But My kindness shall not depart from you,
Nor shall My covenant of peace be removed,"
Says the LORD, who has mercy on you.
—ISAIAH 54:10

Be strong and of good courage, do not fear nor be afraid of them; for the LORD your God, He is the One who goes with you. He will not leave you nor forsake you.
—DEUTERONOMY 31:6

Have you not known?
Have you not heard?
The everlasting God, the LORD,
The Creator of the ends of the earth,
Neither faints nor is weary.
His understanding is unsearchable.
He gives power to the weak,
And to those who have no might He increases
strength.
—ISAIAH 40:28–29

God Challenges
a Father To . . .

Grow in His Christian Walk

The psalmist wrote, "Teach me, O LORD, the way of Your statutes, and I shall keep it to the end" (Psalm 119:33). Left to ourselves, we often don't know which path leads us to life and which path leads us to death. When we don't seek God, we remain in the dark. But God's Word provides us with a searchlight to cut through the darkness and leads us to safety. So spend time in the Word of God and learn how to be the Christian God wants you to be. Get involved in a church and fellowship with other believers. When you desire to grow in Christ, He will provide a way for you to serve Him and be blessed.

Teach me Your way, O Lord;
>*I will walk in Your truth;*
>*Unite my heart to fear Your name.*
>*I will praise You, O Lord my God, with all my
>   heart,*
>*And I will glorify Your name forevermore.*
>>—Psalm 86:11–12

Your word is a lamp to my feet
>*And a light to my path.*
>*I have sworn and confirmed*
>*That I will keep Your righteous judgments.*
>*I am afflicted very much;*
>*Revive me, O Lord, according to Your word.*
>*Accept, I pray, the freewill offerings of my mouth,*
>   *O Lord,*
>*And teach me Your judgments.*
>*My life is continually in my hand,*
>*Yet I do not forget Your law.*
>>—Psalm 119:105–109

Deal Honestly with Others

Proverbs 19:1 says, "Better is the poor who walks in his integrity than one who is perverse in his lips, and is a fool." When you are honest with others, the Lord honors you. Never be afraid to speak openly about your faith to your children and to everyone you meet, even casual acquaintances or strangers on the street. When you choose to be honest with others about what you believe, your character and reputation will grow. As a father, you are a role model for your children. They look up to you and depend on what you say and how other adults perceive you. Let your light shine so that others may see Christ in you.

Do not lie to one another, since you have put off the old man with his deeds, and have put on the new man who is renewed in knowledge according to the image of Him who created him.

—COLOSSIANS 3:9–10

He who would love life
    And see good days,
    Let him refrain his tongue from evil,
    And his lips from speaking deceit.
    Let him turn away from evil and do good;
    Let him seek peace and pursue it.
    For the eyes of the LORD are on the righteous,
    And His ears are open to their prayers;
    But the face of the LORD is against those who do
        evil.

—1 PETER 3:10–12

Ask Forgiveness of Others

One of the most difficult and humbling human experiences is admitting you have wronged people and asking for their forgiveness. Though it may be hard, admitting your wrongdoing gives you a clear conscience and the peace that comes from knowing you did the right thing. And when you humble yourself by seeking amends, your character will grow and God will bless your faithfulness. However, there is no benefit for your spiritual life when you harbor resentment, anger, or grudges in your heart. When you hang onto your pride, God is not honored. Examine your heart today and determine if there is someone you have wronged. Then by God's grace and with His help, seek forgiveness from the one you have hurt.

Blessed is he whose transgression is forgiven, whose sin is covered.

— Psalm 32:1

"And whenever you stand praying, if you have anything against anyone, forgive him, that your Father in heaven may also forgive you your trespasses. But if you do not forgive, neither will your Father in heaven forgive your trespasses."

— Mark 11:25–26

I, therefore, the prisoner of the Lord, beseech you to walk worthy of the calling with which you were called, with all lowliness and gentleness, with longsuffering, bearing with one another in love, endeavoring to keep the unity of the Spirit in the bond of peace.

— Ephesians 4:1–3

Repay no one evil for evil. Have regard for good things in the sight of all men. If it is possible, as much as depends on you, live peaceably with all men.

— Romans 12:17–18

GOD CHALLENGES A FATHER TO . . .
Share His Faith with Others

Romans 10:17 reads, "So then faith comes by hearing, and hearing by the word of God." This is a wonderful promise God gives to His people: He's saying that the more you spend time in His Word, the more your faith will grow and become a part of who you are. Since you are called to share your faith with others, remember that the foundation of a growing faith begins in His Word. Try to spend time with the Lord each day through His holy Scripture, and share the wisdom you glean with others. Get in the habit of being a bold witness for the Lord. The more you share your faith with others, the stronger your own faith becomes.

"Go into all the world and preach the gospel to every creature."

—MARK 16:15

For the word of God is living and powerful, and sharper than any two-edged sword, piercing even to the division of soul and spirit, and of joints and marrow, and is a discerner of the thoughts and intents of the heart.

—HEBREWS 4:12

If you confess with your mouth the Lord Jesus and believe in your heart that God has raised Him from the dead, you will be saved. For with the heart one believes unto righteousness, and with the mouth confession is made unto salvation.

—ROMANS 10:9–10

And let us not grow weary while doing good, for in due season we shall reap if we do not lose heart.

—GALATIANS 6:9

Be Wise with His Finances

As a father, you have been given the enormous responsibility of providing for your family, and how you handle your financial blessings is a direct reflection of your walk with the Lord. Along with providing for your family, God wants you to be a faithful and cheerful giver to the church. In 1 Timothy 6:10, God also challenges you to examine your heart and its motivations concerning money: "For the love of money is a root of all kinds of evil." Simply put, when people are consumed by wealth and the personal power that money provides, they become selfish. So today, commit to being generous with the money the Lord has given you; after all, "It is more blessed to give than to receive" (Acts 20:35).

He who sows sparingly will also reap sparingly, and
he who sows bountifully will also reap bountifully.
So let each one give as he purposes in his heart, not
grudgingly or of necessity; for God loves a cheerful
giver.

—2 Corinthians 9:6–7

Trust in the Lord, and do good;
>*Dwell in the land, and feed on His faithfulness.*
>*Delight yourself also in the Lord,*
>*And He shall give you the desires of your heart.*

—Psalm 37:3–4

"Bring all the tithes into the storehouse,
>*That there may be food in My house,*
>*And try Me now in this,"*
>*Says the Lord of hosts,*
>*"If I will not open for you the windows of heaven*
>*And pour out for you such blessing*
>*That there will not be room enough to receive it."*

—Malachi 3:10

Be an Example to His Christian Brothers

As a Christian, you have been called to be a blessing to your brothers. The apostle Peter painted a clear portrait of the relationship Christian brothers should have: "All of you be of one mind, having compassion for one another; love as brothers, be tenderhearted, be courteous; not returning evil for evil or reviling for reviling, but on the contrary blessing, knowing that you were called to this, that you may inherit a blessing" (1 Peter 3:8–9). According to Peter, being a good Christian brother requires you to step outside of yourself, to think about the struggles of others, and to do good toward them. Put your brothers' needs before your own, and trust that the Lord will provide everything you need.

Two are better than one,
> Because they have a good reward for their labor.
> For if they fall, one will lift up his companion.
> But woe to him who is alone when he falls,
> For he has no one to help him up.
>> —ECCLESIASTES 4:9–10

Be kindly affectionate to one another with brotherly love, in honor giving preference to one another.
>> —ROMANS 12:10

A man who has friends must himself be friendly,
> But there is a friend who sticks closer than a
>> brother.
>>> —PROVERBS 18:24

As iron sharpens iron,
> So a man sharpens the countenance of his friend.
>> —PROVERBS 27:17

A friend loves at all times,
> And a brother is born for adversity.
>> —PROVERBS 17:17

GOD KEEPS A FATHER
SECURE WHEN . . .

He Puts the Lord First in His Life

What kind of relationship do you want to have with Jesus? If your answer is a close relationship, then you must put Him first in your life. God does not wish to be second, third, or last; He wants to be the number-one priority in your life. When the Lord is first in your life, you will instinctively bring your burdens to Him and discover His peace. When He is first, the Spirit will guide you and protect you as you face trials and temptations. God gives you this promise when you put Him first in your life: "Trust in the LORD with all your heart, and lean not on your own understanding; in all your ways acknowledge Him, and He shall direct your paths" (Proverbs 3:5–6).

My son, if you receive my words,
 And treasure my commands within you,
 So that you incline your ear to wisdom,
 And apply your heart to understanding;
 Yes, if you cry out for discernment,
 And lift up your voice for understanding,
 If you seek her as silver,
 And search for her as for hidden treasures;
 Then you will understand the fear of the LORD,
 And find the knowledge of God.

—PROVERBS 2:1–5

I will love You, O LORD, my strength.
 The LORD is my rock and my fortress and my
  deliverer;
 My God, my strength, in whom I will trust;
 My shield and the horn of my salvation, my
  stronghold.
 I will call upon the LORD, who is worthy to be
  praised;
 So shall I be saved from my enemies.

—PSALM 18:1–3

He Changes Jobs

Changing jobs can be unsettling, and on the cusp of this change, you may be assailed with doubts such as whether you will like what you are doing, whether you will succeed with this new company, or whether you will fit into their culture. When panic arises, take all of your doubts and concerns to the Lord in prayer and leave them there. The Lord desires for you to be successful and happy in whatever you choose to do. And when you walk closely with Him and allow Him to be the center of your life, God will bless you, and the Holy Spirit will guide you as you seek to bring glory to Him.

"Therefore I say to you, do not worry about your life, what you will eat or what you will drink; nor about your body, what you will put on. Is not life more than food and the body more than clothing? Look at the birds of the air, for they neither sow nor reap nor gather into barns; yet your heavenly Father feeds them. Are you not of more value than they? Which of you by worrying can add one cubit to his stature?"

—MATTHEW 6:25–27

Be anxious for nothing, but in everything by prayer and supplication, with thanksgiving, let your requests be made known to God; and the peace of God, which surpasses all understanding, will guard your hearts and minds through Christ Jesus.

—PHILIPPIANS 4:6–7

"Ask, and it will be given to you; seek, and you will find; knock, and it will be opened to you."

—MATTHEW 7:7

Worry and Doubt Threaten His Well-Being

Worry, fear, and doubt are Satan's favorite seeds to sow. In fact, they are the most effective tools he uses to create weakness in your faith walk because they paralyze you in your working for God's kingdom. When you are faced with worry and doubt about your circumstances, take them to the Lord; He has promised never to leave you nor forsake you, and He will give you the confidence to handle whatever Satan puts in front of you. The Lord is your protector, and in Him you have everything you need to live securely and confidently. Remember, God will keep you in perfect peace when your mind is stayed on Him (Isaiah 26:3).

The work of righteousness will be peace,
And the effect of righteousness, quietness and
assurance forever.

—Isaiah 32:17

You will keep him in perfect peace,
Whose mind is stayed on You,
Because he trusts in You.

—Isaiah 26:3

"Fear not, for I am with you;
Be not dismayed, for I am your God.
I will strengthen you,
Yes, I will help you,
I will uphold you with My righteous right hand."

—Isaiah 41:10

His Family Faces Enemies

You live in a fallen world. Unfortunately, it is inevitable that at some point, your family will encounter enemies of the Lord. But when your family faces these enemies, you will not face them alone; God will be standing beside you, protecting you and providing shelter in His abiding presence. And the Lord won't send you into the battle unarmed; Ephesians 6 describes the spiritual armor He gives you to put on as you face fiery darts from the evil one. No matter the battles you face, God will guide you and see you safely to the other side. Walk faithfully with the Lord, and He will protect you.

Be strong and of good courage, do not fear nor be afraid of them; for the LORD your God, He is the One who goes with you. He will not leave you nor forsake you.

—DEUTERONOMY 31:6

The eternal God is your refuge,
     And underneath are the everlasting arms;
     He will thrust out the enemy from before you,
     And will say, "Destroy!"

—DEUTERONOMY 33:27

Put on the whole armor of God, that you may be able to stand against the wiles of the devil. For we do not wrestle against flesh and blood, but against principalities, against powers, against the rulers of the darkness of this age, against spiritual hosts of wickedness in the heavenly places. Therefore take up the whole armor of God, that you may be able to withstand in the evil day, and having done all, to stand.

—EPHESIANS 6:11–13

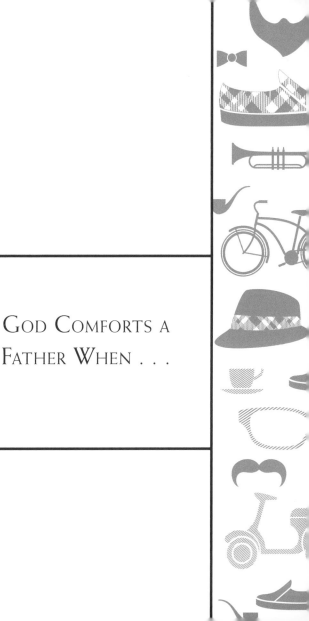

GOD COMFORTS A
FATHER WHEN . . .

His Loved Ones Are Ill

Being sensitive to the needs of your children is part of what it means to be a good father, particularly if your child is ill and in need of healing. Whether you are facing a stomachache or something worse, having a sick child can be a frightening time for any parent because so much of your child's healing is out of your control. When you feel anxious, the Word of God urges you to take your concerns to the Lord in prayer to receive healing, comfort, and strength. Psalm 41:3 says, "The Lord will strengthen him on his bed of illness; You will sustain him on his sickbed." When you take the illness of your child to the Lord in prayer, He will listen and come to your aid.

*Is anyone among you sick? Let him call for the elders
of the church, and let them pray over him, anointing
him with oil in the name of the Lord. And the prayer
of faith will save the sick, and the Lord will raise him
up. And if he has committed sins, he will be forgiven.
Confess your trespasses to one another, and pray for
one another, that you may be healed. The effective,
fervent prayer of a righteous man avails much.*

—James 5:14–16

Heal me, O Lord, and I shall be healed;
    Save me, and I shall be saved,
    For You are my praise.

—Jeremiah 17:14

His Loved Ones Don't Understand Him

One of the most frustrating experiences is trying to convey your thoughts to others and they don't understand what you're saying or even become unnecessarily offended. When others do not seem to understand you, the Bible says you should treat them with kindness and patience anyway. When you answer their hard words with a gentle reply, walls of discord will fall, and your attitude will be affected in a positive way toward that person. Just as Christ has been gracious and kind toward you, be kind to anyone with whom you have a disagreement.

Let love be without hypocrisy. Abhor what is evil. Cling to what is good. Be kindly affectionate to one another with brotherly love, in honor giving preference to one another.

—Romans 12:9–10

A soft answer turns away wrath,
*   But a harsh word stirs up anger.*

—Proverbs 15:1

"Blessed are you when they revile and persecute you, and say all kinds of evil against you falsely for My sake. Rejoice and be exceedingly glad, for great is your reward in heaven, for so they persecuted the prophets who were before you."

—Matthew 5:11–12

GOD COMFORTS A FATHER WHEN . . .

He Must Discipline His Loved Ones

When you have to discipline your children, you as a parent must bear the responsibility, no matter how painful, because in the long run providing discipline is the best way your child will learn how to behave and mature into a responsible adult. Proverbs 13:24 says, "He who spares his rod hates his son, but he who loves him disciplines him promptly." As difficult as it is to punish your children, they need correction and direction as they are growing up. Do not hesitate to correct your children when they do something that you know is wrong. As they mature and become adults, your children will thank you for showing them how they should act and talk.

*My son, do not despise the chastening of the L*ORD,
    Nor detest His correction;
    *For whom the L*ORD *loves He corrects,*
    Just as a father the son in whom he delights.
                    —PROVERBS 3:11–12

Furthermore, we have had human fathers who corrected us, and we paid them respect. Shall we not much more readily be in subjection to the Father of spirits and live? For they indeed for a few days chastened us as seemed best to them, but He for our profit, that we may be partakers of His holiness. Now no chastening seems to be joyful for the present, but painful; nevertheless, afterward it yields the peaceable fruit of righteousness to those who have been trained by it.
                    —HEBREWS 12:9–11

My son, keep my words,
    And treasure my commands within you.
    Keep my commands and live,
    And my law as the apple of your eye.
                    —PROVERBS 7:1–2

GOD'S LOVE IS WITH A FATHER WHEN . . .

He Brings His Problems to the Lord

Some days your problems may weigh so heavily that it is as if someone has hung a cinderblock around your chest. But you don't have to bear these problems alone. God loves you and cares about you more than you can imagine. He has promised never to leave you nor forsake you when you have a problem; He is always waiting to listen to your dilemma. Malachi 3:16 says, "Then those who feared the Lord spoke to one another, and the Lord listened and heard them." The Lord is ever present to hear your problems, and His Spirit will guide you whenever you face something difficult. Nothing is too great or impossible for God. Take your burdens to the Lord, and leave them there.

"For the eyes of the LORD are on the righteous,
    And His ears are open to their prayers;
    But the face of the LORD is against those who do
        evil."

And who is he who will harm you if you become followers of what is good? But even if you should suffer for righteousness' sake, you are blessed. "And do not be afraid of their threats, nor be troubled." But sanctify the Lord God in your hearts, and always be ready to give a defense to everyone who asks you a reason for the hope that is in you, with meekness and fear.

—1 PETER 3:12–15

But Jesus looked at them and said to them, "With men this is impossible, but with God all things are possible."

—MATTHEW 19:26

Be strong and of good courage, do not fear nor be afraid of them; for the LORD your God, He is the One who goes with you. He will not leave you nor forsake you.

—DEUTERONOMY 31:6

He Relies on the Lord to Guide His Children

As a father, it is really important to come to the Lord for guidance—particularly when it comes to your children. They are precious gifts who have been given to you to educate, raise, and place within their hearts the confidence that they are loved by you and by the Lord. When they see the Lord reflected in your lifestyle, they learn more about faith and about God. Give thought to how you can give your children a firm foundation in the Lord through your words and actions. Play with them, listen to them, and pray with them. Demonstrate your love for them. Make sure they can see that you put Christ first in your life.

When you roam, they will lead you;
 When you sleep, they will keep you;
 And when you awake, they will speak with you.
 For the commandment is a lamp,
 And the law a light;
 Reproofs of instruction are the way of life.

        —Proverbs 6:22–23

"I will go before you
 And make the crooked places straight. . . .
 I will give you the treasures of darkness
 And hidden riches of secret places,
 That you may know that I, the Lord,
 Who call you by your name,
 Am the God of Israel."

        —Isaiah 45:2–3

He Forgives His Children

There's nothing like the rush of joy and relief you feel when you choose to forgive your children. The wall of anger and frustration that has been slowly building is torn down and in its place comes the gentle love and grace that you should have for your children. When you contemplate forgiveness, think to yourself, *God has forgiven me of all my sins and loves me just the way I am. If Christ has forgiven me, shouldn't I forgive my child?* If you want to create a bond of love between you and your children, then forgive them openly and tell how much they mean to you and how deep is your love for them.

The Lord is merciful and gracious,
>   Slow to anger, and abounding in mercy.
>   He will not always strive with us,
>   Nor will He keep His anger forever.
>   He has not dealt with us according to our sins,
>   Nor punished us according to our iniquities.
>   For as the heavens are high above the earth,
>   So great is His mercy toward those who fear Him;
>   As far as the east is from the west,
>   So far has He removed our transgressions from us.
>   —PSALM 103:8–12

"For if you forgive men their trespasses, your heavenly Father will also forgive you."

>   —MATTHEW 6:14

He Learns to Trust in the Lord

When you learn to trust in the Lord with all of your heart, you make a great leap of faith. In fact, placing your trust in God is the beginning of giving Him the proper place in your life. Jesus paid the ultimate price for your sin, and He deserves your trust. When you put your life in His hands, the barriers that keep you from having an intimate relationship with God come down, and you are free to live in His presence every moment of every day. Let the Spirit of the Lord guide you into a deeper relationship with Christ. If you do this, you and all those you come in contact with will be blessed.

Every word of God is pure;
He is a shield to those who put their trust in Him.

—Proverbs 30:5

My soul, wait silently for God alone,
For my expectation is from Him.
He only is my rock and my salvation;
He is my defense;
I shall not be moved.
In God is my salvation and my glory;
The rock of my strength,
And my refuge, is in God.
Trust in Him at all times, you people;
Pour out your heart before Him;
God is a refuge for us.

—Psalm 62:5–8

Every good gift and every perfect gift is from above,
and comes down from the Father of lights, with whom
there is no variation or shadow of turning.

—James 1:17

GOD REJOICES
WHEN . . .

His Family Anticipates
the Lord's Return

L iving with anticipation completely changes your view of the present; the least important things are stripped away, while you become laser-focused on what you deem most important. And when you live as if the Lord is coming back at any moment, your anticipation will help grow a deep, personal relationship with the Lord. Revelation 3:20 says, "Behold, I stand at the door and knock. If anyone hears My voice and opens the door, I will come in to him and dine with him, and he with Me." You have an open invitation to enjoy a close relationship with the Lord, so talk to your family often about what the return of Jesus means for you today.

The LORD has established His throne in heaven,
And His kingdom rules over all.

—PSALM 103:19

It is good that one should hope and wait quietly
For the salvation of the LORD.

—LAMENTATIONS 3:26

I wait for the LORD, my soul waits,
And in His word I do hope.
My soul waits for the Lord
More than those who watch for the morning—
Yes, more than those who watch for the morning.

—PSALM 130:5–6

He Dedicates His Children to the Lord

Dedicating your children to God is a big step for any father. Because when you pledge to become your child's faith guide, you take the responsibility for nurturing and providing guidance in his or her Christian life. Consistency will help your child develop his or her faith in a steady way. Seek the Lord daily in prayer, asking that you will be an example of Christian character that will cause your child to want to walk with the Lord. Remember to tell your children that our Father God acts for our benefit in ways that we cannot always understand. He molds us and shapes us in ways that sometimes hurt, but He always deals with us in love.

"For I will pour water on him who is thirsty,
And floods on the dry ground;
I will pour My Spirit on your descendants,
And My blessing on your offspring."

—Isaiah 44:3

But now, O Lord,
You are our Father;
We are the clay, and You our potter;
And all we are the work of Your hand.

—Isaiah 64:8

And now, little children, abide in Him, that when He
appears, we may have confidence and not be ashamed
before Him at His coming.

—1 John 2:28

Hear, my son, and receive my sayings,
And the years of your life will be many.
I have taught you in the way of wisdom;
I have led you in right paths.

—Proverbs 4:10–11

He Trusts the Lord and Waits for the Lord's Answers

Waiting on God takes patience, sometimes more than we think we have to give. When trouble and confusion fill your life, sometimes you just want to get your answers immediately. Trusting in God is a learning experience that comes to you when you turn your life over to the Lord and walk with Him every day. No matter where you travel, no matter what challenges you face, God goes before you, inviting you to hand your doubts and fears to Him. If you just trust in Him and wait patiently for His answers, He will comfort you and give you strength to keep going.

Every word of God is pure;
    He is a shield to those who put their trust in Him.

            —Proverbs 30:5

Do not be deceived, my beloved brethren. Every good gift and every perfect gift is from above, and comes down from the Father of lights, with whom there is no variation or shadow of turning.

            —James 1:16–17

Be still, and know that I am God.

            —Psalm 46:10

Rest in the Lord, and wait patiently for Him;
    Do not fret because of him who prospers in his
        way,
    Because of the man who brings wicked schemes
        to pass. . . .
    But those who wait on the Lord,
    They shall inherit the earth.

            —Psalm 37:7, 9

He Teaches His Children to Show Mercy to Others

The Bible speaks in many places about the mercy of the Lord. In Luke 6:36–37, Jesus said, "Therefore be merciful, just as your Father also is merciful. Judge not, and you shall not be judged. Condemn not, and you shall not be condemned. Forgive, and you will be forgiven." When you teach your children to show mercy to others, you are teaching them to be more like Jesus. He demonstrated His great mercy for you when you didn't deserve it. When you treat others how you would like to be treated, you are a living example of the Christian experience. People who have received mercy—and every Christian has—ought to be quick to show mercy to others.

*Let nothing be done through selfish ambition or
conceit, but in lowliness of mind let each esteem others
better than himself. Let each of you look out not only
for his own interests, but also for the interests of others.*
—Philippians 2:3–4

*"But love your enemies, do good, and lend, hoping for
nothing in return; and your reward will be great, and
you will be sons of the Most High. For He is kind to
the unthankful and evil. Therefore be merciful, just as
your Father also is merciful. Judge not, and you shall
not be judged. Condemn not, and you shall not be
condemned. Forgive, and you will be forgiven. Give,
and it will be given to you: good measure, pressed
down, shaken together, and running over will be put
into your bosom."*
—Luke 6:35–38

*And let us not grow weary while doing good, for in due
season we shall reap if we do not lose heart.*
—Galatians 6:9

GOD GIVES A FATHER
STRENGTH WHEN . . .

He Comforts His Loved Ones

In times of trouble, God promises to be with you. He is always there to listen; He comforts you amid your difficulties and gives you the peace that passes all understanding. The Lord is your example for helping your children when they are hurting. When you reach out in love and comfort your children, you are doing God's will for the ones He has given you to raise. The love that you give to your children will last for a lifetime, and it is worth more than anything you might purchase for them. When you show love to your children, you draw them closer to you and provide an opportunity to share the love of Christ.

*Blessed be the God and Father of our Lord Jesus Christ,
the Father of mercies and God of all comfort, who comforts us in all our tribulation, that we may be able to
comfort those who are in any trouble, with the comfort
with which we ourselves are comforted by God.*

—2 Corinthians 1:3–4

*Yea, though I walk through the valley of the shadow of
death,*

> *I will fear no evil;*
> *For You are with me;*
> *Your rod and Your staff, they comfort me.*
> *You prepare a table before me in the presence of*
>   *my enemies;*
> *You anoint my head with oil;*
> *My cup runs over.*
> *Surely goodness and mercy shall follow me*
> *All the days of my life;*
> *And I will dwell in the house of the Lord*
> *Forever.*

—Psalm 23:4–6

Loved Ones Die

The loss of a loved one is a tragedy for anyone to experience. You may struggle to understand why God would take someone, especially if that someone happens to be young. On this side of heaven, you may never understand how "all things work together for good" for God's children—certainly not all things in and of themselves are good, but God is able to bring good out of something that's bad (Romans 8:28). To stand firm in your faith, you must trust that God is in control even when it seems like He isn't. As difficult as it may be, you can rest in the knowledge that your loved one is now in the care of Jesus and live with peace in your heart. You can be reassured that someday you will be reunited with those you have lost.

The Lord is near to those who have a broken heart.
—Psalm 34:18

"When you pass through the waters, I will be with you;
And through the rivers, they shall not overflow
you.
When you walk through the fire, you shall not be
burned,
Nor shall the flame scorch you.
For I am the Lord your God,
The Holy One of Israel, your Savior."
—Isaiah 43:2–3

For I am persuaded that neither death nor life, nor
angels nor principalities nor powers, nor things present
nor things to come, nor height nor depth, nor any
other created thing, shall be able to separate us from
the love of God which is in Christ Jesus our Lord.
—Romans 8:38–39

GOD GIVES A FATHER STRENGTH WHEN . . .

He Is Angry and Needs Peace

We all get angry sometimes, and anger is a valid emotion. But controlling your words and actions when your emotions run hot is essential for every father. The Bible reminds you that "He who is slow to anger is better than the mighty" (Proverbs 16:32). Whether you realize it or not, your children are watching you, and how you conduct yourself when you're upset will influence how they learn to deal with anger. So when you encounter a tough situation, try to think twice before you react in anger. God's peace comes when you take your anger to Him and leave it there. Don't forget: little eyes are always watching and taking their cues from you, their father.

So then, my beloved brethren, let every man be swift to hear, slow to speak, slow to wrath; for the wrath of man does not produce the righteousness of God.

—JAMES 1:19–20

He who is slow to anger is better than the mighty,
*   And he who rules his spirit than he who takes a city.*

—PROVERBS 16:32

Let your speech always be with grace, seasoned with salt, that you may know how you ought to answer each one.

—COLOSSIANS 4:6

Cease from anger, and forsake wrath;
*   Do not fret—it only causes harm.*

—PSALM 37:8

Let all bitterness, wrath, anger, clamor, and evil speaking be put away from you, with all malice.

—EPHESIANS 4:31

His Children Disobey Him

Sometimes your children disappoint you with disobedience. It is inevitable; everyone makes mistakes, and an important part of growing up is learning what is right and wrong. How you handle these situations will impact your relationship with your children and your ability to influence them in positive ways. You should correct your children through love, and make sure they do not mistake discipline for rejection. After you have disciplined your children, make it clear to them that you love them very much, and that you do not love them any less. Explain that you only want the best for them, which is why you corrected their behavior. Even though it's hard, disciplining your children is best for both the child and the parent in the long run.

Children, obey your parents in the Lord, for this is right . . . . And you, fathers, do not provoke your children to wrath, but bring them up in the training and admonition of the Lord.

—EPHESIANS 6:1, 4

"If his sons forsake My law
And do not walk in My judgments,
If they break My statutes
And do not keep My commandments,
Then I will punish their transgression with the rod,
And their iniquity with stripes.
Nevertheless My lovingkindness I will not utterly
take from him,
Nor allow My faithfulness to fail.
My covenant I will not break,
Nor alter the word that has gone out of My lips."

—PSALM 89:30–34

Foolishness is bound up in the heart of a child;
The rod of correction will drive it far from him.

—PROVERBS 22:15

His Family Grows Apart

Creating a dynamic of peace among your family members is essential to family unity and preventing your loved ones from growing apart. There are two keys to keeping the family together. One is forgiveness. Whenever you fight with a family member, don't go to bed angry; be the first to seek forgiveness and heal the wound that was created. The second key is love. When you make a habit of showing love and affection to the members of your family, your actions will cover many wrongs. Be slow to anger and quick to tell your family how much they mean to you. Develop the attitude that growing apart is never an option.

God sets the solitary in families;
    He brings out those who are bound into
        prosperity;
    But the rebellious dwell in a dry land.
                                —PSALM 68:6

A wrathful man stirs up strife,
    But he who is slow to anger allays contention.
                                —PROVERBS 15:18

"Blessed are the peacemakers,
    For they shall be called sons of God."
                                —MATTHEW 5:9

"Be angry, and do not sin": do not let the sun go down
on your wrath. . . . Let all bitterness, wrath, anger,
clamor, and evil speaking be put away from you, with
all malice. And be kind to one another, tenderhearted,
forgiving one another, even as God in Christ forgave
you.
                                —EPHESIANS 4:26, 31–32

God Asks a
Father To . . .

GOD ASKS A FATHER TO . . .

Witness to the Lost

You communicate by what you say and don't say, by what you do and fail to do. A father who never reads the Bible conveys that he is smart enough to make his own decisions without any input from God. The children who never see their parents praying learn that trials and tribulations can be handled without any direction from the Lord. On the other hand, when a father says, "We are going to trust the Lord to provide what we need," he declares that God can be trusted in every facet of life. Just as you show your faith to your children, show your faith to the lost. Your witness could be the only Jesus they will ever see or hear.

"Go therefore and make disciples of all the nations, baptizing them in the name of the Father and of the Son and of the Holy Spirit, teaching them to observe all things that I have commanded you; and lo, I am with you always, even to the end of the age."

—Matthew 28:19–20

Therefore God also has highly exalted Him and given Him the name which is above every name, that at the name of Jesus every knee should bow, of those in heaven, and of those on earth, and of those under the earth, and that every tongue should confess that Jesus Christ is Lord, to the glory of God the Father.

—Philippians 2:9–11

"Let your light so shine before men, that they may see your good works and glorify your Father in heaven."

—Matthew 5:16

Love His Neighbors

In Galatians 5:14, Paul reminds Christians of one of their most important tasks: "You shall love your neighbor as yourself." Your neighbor is not confined to the person living next door; *everyone* is your neighbor. And how you treat your neighbor is a reflection of what kind of relationship you have with the Lord. Think about how you act when you love someone: you are kind and caring, showing them goodness, gentleness, and faithfulness. You may disagree with someone you love, but you don't let the disagreement color your behavior toward them—you love them anyway. So let your light shine, showing your neighbors that same love. When you do, they will see Jesus in you.

Jesus said to him, "'You shall love the Lord *your God with all your heart, with all your soul, and with all your mind.' This is the first and great commandment. And the second is like it: 'You shall love your neighbor as yourself.'"*

—Matthew 22:37–39

"'These are the things you shall do:
    Speak each man the truth to his neighbor;
    Give judgment in your gates for truth, justice,
        and peace;
    Let none of you think evil in your heart against
        your neighbor;
    And do not love a false oath.
    For all these are things that I hate,'
    Says the Lord*."*

—Zechariah 8:16–17

"If you want to enter into life, keep the commandments . . . 'Honor your father and your mother,' and, 'You shall love your neighbor as yourself.'"

—Matthew 19:17, 19

Instruct His Children in the Word

One of the greatest responsibilities of a father is to make sure that his children understand God's Word and help them live with the love of Christ in their hearts. It's important to guide your child to a close relationship with the Lord very early in life. When you plant the seed of God's Word early, it will take root, grow, and become a part of them. As your children learn what it means to live for Christ daily, their relationship with God will bear much fruit as they mature and surrender their lives to the Lord.

Hear, my children, the instruction of a father,
    And give attention to know understanding;
    For I give you good doctrine:
    Do not forsake my law.
    When I was my father's son,
    Tender and the only one in the sight of my
        mother,
    He also taught me, and said to me:
    "Let your heart retain my words;
    Keep my commands, and live.
    Get wisdom! Get understanding!
    Do not forget, nor turn away from the words of
        my mouth.
    Do not forsake her, and she will preserve you;
    Love her, and she will keep you. . . ."
    My son, give attention to my words;
    Incline your ear to my sayings.
    Do not let them depart from your eyes;
    Keep them in the midst of your heart;
    For they are life to those who find them.
                —PROVERBS 4:1–6, 20–22

Trust God

As a father, you will face many decisions that will affect the lives of your family. Trusting in God to lead you daily is one of the wisest things you will ever do. God loves you with an everlasting love and cares deeply about you and your family. He has marvelous plans for all of you and can work everything together for your good. Therefore, it is essential that you trust in the Lord with all of your heart. When you lean on your heavenly Father for knowledge, understanding, and wisdom, He will guide you and give you the direction you need to be the father God has called you to be.

Trust in the LORD with all your heart,
> *And lean not on your own understanding;*
> *In all your ways acknowledge Him,*
> *And He shall direct your paths.*
>> —PROVERBS 3:5–6

The LORD is my rock and my fortress and my deliverer;
> *The God of my strength, in whom I will trust;*
> *My shield and the horn of my salvation,*
> *My stronghold and my refuge;*
> *My Savior, You save me from violence.*
>> —2 SAMUEL 22:2–3

Trust in the LORD, and do good;
> *Dwell in the land, and feed on His faithfulness.*
> *Delight yourself also in the LORD,*
> *And He shall give you the desires of your heart.*
> *Commit your way to the LORD,*
> *Trust also in Him,*
> *And He shall bring it to pass.*
>> —PSALM 37:3–5

Teach His Children Gratitude

One of the most important lessons your children can learn at a young age is to be thankful, no matter what comes their way. When you instill a sense of gratitude in the hearts of your children, you are giving them a firm foundation to live a Christ-centered life. The Bible encourages you to give thanks in everything. When you have a thankful attitude, you can treat a negative situation as though it is an opportunity; you can handle the trials of life with grace. Having an attitude of gratitude can help you live in such a way that your heavenly Father is honored.

Let your conduct be without covetousness; be content
with such things as you have. For He Himself has
said, "I will never leave you nor forsake you."

—HEBREWS 13:5

Sing praise to the LORD, you saints of His,
    And give thanks at the remembrance of His holy
        name.
    For His anger is but for a moment,
    His favor is for life;
    Weeping may endure for a night,
    But joy comes in the morning.

—PSALM 30:4–5

Make a joyful shout to the LORD, all you lands!
    Serve the LORD with gladness;
    Come before His presence with singing.

—PSALM 100:1–2

GOD ASKS A FATHER TO...

Show Kindness to His Family

One of the best ways to demonstrate your love for your family is to show them kindness, which you can do in a variety of ways: through your words, your thoughts, and your actions. Kindness is a fruit of the Spirit, a natural outpouring of the love that the Lord has given you. How does that happen? As you live by the Spirit, you will think of others' needs before your own, and your loving thoughts will drive loving actions. Jesus wants you to exhibit kindness to your family and to others. Think about how you've been living. Do you consistently show kindness to your loved ones? If not, pray that the Lord will fill your thoughts with His love so that you will live out His love more intentionally.

Let all bitterness, wrath, anger, clamor, and evil speaking be put away from you, with all malice. And be kind to one another, tenderhearted, forgiving one another, even as God in Christ forgave you.

—Ephesians 4:31–32

As you know how we exhorted, and comforted, and charged every one of you, as a father does his own children, that you would walk worthy of God who calls you into His own kingdom and glory.

—1 Thessalonians 2:11–12

"Or what man is there among you who, if his son asks for bread, will give him a stone? Or if he asks for a fish, will he give him a serpent? If you then, being evil, know how to give good gifts to your children, how much more will your Father who is in heaven give good things to those who ask Him!"

—Matthew 7:9–11

GOD FREELY GIVES
TO A FATHER . . .

Eternal Hope for Life

The Bible says in Psalm 33:18, "Behold, the eye of the LORD is on those who fear Him, on those who hope in His mercy." You have a hope that has been planted in your heart by God. You look forward to spending time with Him in heaven. When you talk openly about the hope of eternal life with your children, you are planting the seed of salvation in their hearts. Praise the Lord and give thanks for His marvelous gift of eternal life. You are blessed to have a heavenly Father who forgives your sins, makes you more like Himself, and has made a home for you in heaven with Him.

*For God did not appoint us to wrath, but to obtain
salvation through our Lord Jesus Christ, who died
for us, that whether we wake or sleep, we should live
together with Him. Therefore comfort each other and
edify one another, just as you also are doing.*

—1 Thessalonians 5:9–11

*Blessed be the God and Father of our Lord Jesus
Christ, who according to His abundant mercy has
begotten us again to a living hope through the resur-
rection of Jesus Christ from the dead, to an inheritance
incorruptible and undefiled and that does not fade
away, reserved in heaven for you, who are kept by the
power of God through faith for salvation ready to be
revealed in the last time.*

—1 Peter 1:3–5

*The Spirit Himself bears witness with our spirit that
we are children of God, and if children, then heirs—
heirs of God and joint heirs with Christ.*

—Romans 8:16–17

Wisdom for Each Day

The Lord urges you to pay attention to His wisdom, and the best place to find the wisdom of the Lord is in His Word. As a father and spiritual leader, it is crucial for you to seek His wisdom diligently. The book of Proverbs repeatedly tells of the importance of gaining wisdom, which is far more valuable than any possession one could hope to own. Why? Because you cannot put a price tag on a well-lived life, one that is lived for the Lord. When you learn to share God's wisdom from His Word with your children, they will listen and learn what it means to walk with God each day.

My son, pay attention to my wisdom;
Lend your ear to my understanding,
That you may preserve discretion,
And your lips may keep knowledge.

—Proverbs 5:1–2

If any of you lacks wisdom, let him ask of God, who
gives to all liberally and without reproach, and it
will be given to him. But let him ask in faith, with no
doubting, for he who doubts is like a wave of the sea
driven and tossed by the wind.

—James 1:5–6

Happy is the man who finds wisdom,
And the man who gains understanding;
For her proceeds are better than the profits of
silver,
And her gain than fine gold.
She is more precious than rubies,
And all the things you may desire cannot
compare with her.

—Proverbs 3:13–15

Victory over Sin

How you live is important in the eyes of the Lord; what you say and do reflects who you are and what you are becoming, which is hopefully a strong ambassador for Him. Throughout the Bible, the Lord clearly says that He wants you to abide in Him and draw near to Him. When you obey God's Word, you will bear much fruit and your life will glorify Him. When you teach your children to live for Christ, you are giving them the best gift: a pathway to freedom from sin and a life filled with the presence of God. Plant the love of Jesus Christ within the hearts of your children. It is the way to life everlasting.

Therefore, if anyone is in Christ, he is a new creation; old things have passed away; behold, all things have become new. Now all things are of God, who has reconciled us to Himself through Jesus Christ, and has given us the ministry of reconciliation, that is, that God was in Christ reconciling the world to Himself, not imputing their trespasses to them, and has committed to us the word of reconciliation.

—2 Corinthians 5:17–19

This is the message which we have heard from Him and declare to you, that God is light and in Him is no darkness at all. If we say that we have fellowship with Him, and walk in darkness, we lie and do not practice the truth. But if we walk in the light as He is in the light, we have fellowship with one another, and the blood of Jesus Christ His Son cleanses us from all sin.

—1 John 1:5–7

Little children, let no one deceive you. He who practices righteousness is righteous, just as He is righteous.

—1 John 3:7

GOD FREELY GIVES TO A FATHER . . .

Peace in Troubled Times

When a crisis comes into your life, your first response might be to turn inward and try to solve the problem on your own. But as tempting as it is for you to take matters into your own hands, you don't have to bear your burdens alone; Jesus stands waiting for you to come to Him and ask for His help. When you are faced with troubled times, God has promised to give you His peace. You can trust in the Lord to give you the strength, patience, and understanding to help you handle any situation you may encounter. God cares for you and wants the best for you in every circumstance, so take your problems to Him and leave them there.

I will bless the LORD at all times;
His praise shall continually be in my mouth.
My soul shall make its boast in the LORD;
The humble shall hear of it and be glad.
Oh, magnify the LORD with me,
And let us exalt His name together.
I sought the LORD, and He heard me,
And delivered me from all my fears.
They looked to Him and were radiant,
And their faces were not ashamed.
This poor man cried out, and the LORD heard him,
And saved him out of all his troubles.
The angel of the LORD encamps all around those
who fear Him,
And delivers them.
Oh, taste and see that the LORD is good;
Blessed is the man who trusts in Him!

—PSALM 34:1–8

Courage to Be a Man of Integrity

As a father and a Christian, character development and living with integrity are what matter most. Your children are always watching your reactions and listening to your words—whether good or bad. When you allow Christ to live through you, you will exhibit godly character and boldly proclaim His name. Proverbs 20:7 says, "The righteous man walks in his integrity; his children are blessed after him." Live in such a way that you honor God in all that you say and do, so that your children will want to follow in your footsteps. Remember: you are planting seeds that will bear fruit long after you are gone.

Dishonest scales are an abomination to the L<small>ORD</small>,
But a just weight is His delight.
When pride comes, then comes shame;
But with the humble is wisdom.
The integrity of the upright will guide them,
But the perversity of the unfaithful will
destroy them.

—P<small>ROVERBS</small> 11:1–3

The righteous man walks in his integrity;
His children are blessed after him.

—P<small>ROVERBS</small> 20:7

The L<small>ORD</small> shall judge the peoples;
Judge me, O L<small>ORD</small>, according to my
righteousness,
And according to my integrity within me.

—P<small>SALM</small> 7:8

GOD'S WISDOM TO
BLESS YOUR FAMILY . . .

With Love

How fortunate you are that "the love of God has been poured out in our hearts by the Holy Spirit" (Romans 5:5). The Lord is walking with you each and every day. He loves you with an everlasting love, and there is nothing you can do that will stop Him from loving you. So give thanks and be of good courage, for the Lord is your rock and your salvation and in Him you have life (Psalm 62:2). You as a father have been blessed with the love of Christ; share that love with your children, and let them know how important it is to have Jesus Christ as their Savior.

*That Christ may dwell in your hearts through faith;
that you, being rooted and grounded in love, may
be able to comprehend with all the saints what is the
width and length and depth and height—to know the
love of Christ which passes knowledge; that you may
be filled with all the fullness of God.*

—Ephesians 3:17–19

*Now hope does not disappoint, because the love of God
has been poured out in our hearts by the Holy Spirit
who was given to us. . . . But God demonstrates His
own love toward us, in that while we were still sinners,
Christ died for us. Much more then, having now been
justified by His blood, we shall be saved from wrath
through Him.*

—Romans 5:5, 7–9

*But God, who is rich in mercy, because of His great
love with which He loved us, even when we were dead
in trespasses, made us alive together with Christ (by
grace you have been saved).*

—Ephesians 2:4–5

With Strength

When God gives you the gift of salvation, He blesses you with the strength of the Holy Spirit. Because you have the Spirit, the Lord is with you to guide you and give you the courage and fortitude you need to handle life's circumstances. Psalm 27:1 says, "The LORD is my light and my salvation; whom shall I fear? The LORD is the strength of my life; of whom shall I be afraid?" You can depend on the Lord to supply all of the strength you will ever need. You just need to place all of your trust in Him and depend on Him every day.

The LORD is my strength and my shield;
My heart trusted in Him, and I am helped;
Therefore my heart greatly rejoices,
And with my song I will praise Him.
The LORD is their strength,
And He is the saving refuge of His anointed.
Save Your people,
And bless Your inheritance;
Shepherd them also,
And bear them up forever.

—Psalm 28:7–9

God is our refuge and strength,
A very present help in trouble.
Therefore we will not fear,
Even though the earth be removed,
And though the mountains be carried into the
midst of the sea;
Though its waters roar and be troubled,
Though the mountains shake with its swelling.

—Psalm 46:1–3

With Joy

God desires for you to have a joyful life filled with happiness. Psalm 30:5 says, "For His anger is but for a moment, His favor is for life; weeping may endure for a night, but joy comes in the morning." Did you know that He has given you a plan to achieve that joy? When you choose to live in the center of God's will, He gives you joy that you want to share. With joy comes great confidence that God covers you with His love. Let the joy of the Lord fill your heart as you walk with Him through life's ups and downs.

But let all those rejoice who put their trust in You;
> Let them ever shout for joy, because You defend
> > them;
> Let those also who love Your name
> Be joyful in You.
> For You, O LORD, will bless the righteous;
> With favor You will surround him as with a
> > shield.

—PSALM 5:11–12

"If you keep My commandments, you will abide in My love, just as I have kept My Father's commandments and abide in His love. These things I have spoken to you, that My joy may remain in you, and that your joy may be full."

—JOHN 15:10–11

You will show me the path of life;
> In Your presence is fullness of joy;
> At Your right hand are pleasures forevermore.

—PSALM 16:11

With Fruitfulness

When you consider the fruit of the Spirit, you gain a better understanding of the great love God has lavished on you, and the results of that great love. When you seek to serve the Lord and open your heart to His leading, He will produce good fruit in your life. As a father, show your children how the Lord is working in your life by showing them how to be kind and good and how to exhibit the other fruit of the Spirit. When children catch a glimpse of the Spirit living through you, it will make following Jesus more real and more desirable to them.

*But the fruit of the Spirit is love, joy, peace, longsuf-
fering, kindness, goodness, faithfulness, gentleness,
self-control. Against such there is no law. And those
who are Christ's have crucified the flesh with its
passions and desires. If we live in the Spirit, let us also
walk in the Spirit.*

—GALATIANS 5:22–25

*For this reason we also, since the day we heard it, do not
cease to pray for you, and to ask that you may be filled
with the knowledge of His will in all wisdom and spiritual understanding; that you may walk worthy of the
Lord, fully pleasing Him, being fruitful in every good
work and increasing in the knowledge of God.*

—COLOSSIANS 1:9–10

*My fruit is better than gold, yes, than fine gold,
        And my revenue than choice silver.
        I traverse the way of righteousness,
        In the midst of the paths of justice,
        That I may cause those who love me to inherit wealth.*

—PROVERBS 8:19–21

With Rest

We live in such a fast-paced world that taking time to rest seems impractical if not impossible. The Bible speaks specifically about this subject. Psalm 37:7–8 says, "Rest in the LORD, and wait patiently for Him." We need to spend time with the Lord and meditate on His Word. When we do that, God restores our strength and renews our perspective. We have been instructed to labor for six days and then rest on the seventh day. If you want to live a sustainable faith that energizes you and blesses others, you will have to learn to rest both physically and spiritually.

"Come to Me, all you who labor and are heavy laden,
and I will give you rest. Take My yoke upon you and
learn from Me, for I am gentle and lowly in heart,
and you will find rest for your souls. For My yoke is
easy and My burden is light."

—MATTHEW 11:28–30

The LORD preserves the simple;
    I was brought low, and He saved me.
    Return to your rest, O my soul,
    For the LORD has dealt bountifully with you.

—PSALM 116:6–7

Rest in the LORD, and wait patiently for Him;
    Do not fret because of him who prospers in his way,
    Because of the man who brings wicked schemes
        to pass.
    Cease from anger, and forsake wrath;
    Do not fret—it only causes harm.

—PSALM 37:7–8

With His Spirit

As Christians, we have been promised the Holy Spirit. John 14:26 says, "But the Helper, the Holy Spirit, whom the Father will send in My name, He will teach you all things, and bring to your remembrance all things that I said to you." You are so blessed to have the Spirit of truth abiding in you. He is there to guide your thoughts and lead you through life so that you might bring honor and glory to your heavenly Father. And God has promised to give you His peace through the Holy Spirit. As a father, pray daily for the Spirit of God to guide you as you seek to be the best father possible.

Beloved, if God so loved us, we also ought to love one another. No one has seen God at any time. If we love one another, God abides in us, and His love has been perfected in us. By this we know that we abide in Him, and He in us, because He has given us of His Spirit.

—1 John 4:11–13

But if the Spirit of Him who raised Jesus from the dead dwells in you, He who raised Christ from the dead will also give life to your mortal bodies through His Spirit who dwells in you.

—Romans 8:10–11

For our gospel did not come to you in word only, but also in power, and in the Holy Spirit and in much assurance, as you know what kind of men we were among you for your sake.

—1 Thessalonians 1:5

With Hope

Your faith and hope are established by the blood of Jesus Christ, who gave Himself for you so that you can be forgiven and granted a new life that lasts forever. First John 3:2–3 says, "When He is revealed, we shall be like Him, for we shall see Him as He is. And everyone who has this hope in Him purifies himself, just as He is pure." One day, you will exchange your worn-out, weak body for a new model patterned after Jesus' resurrected body—strong, ageless, free of all sin, and completely at home in the holy presence of God. So have hope! Your future with God is incredibly bright.

Now may the God of hope fill you with all joy and peace in believing, that you may abound in hope by the power of the Holy Spirit.

—ROMANS 15:13

For I consider that the sufferings of this present time are not worthy to be compared with the glory which shall be revealed in us. For the earnest expectation of the creation eagerly waits for the revealing of the sons of God. . . . For we were saved in this hope, but hope that is seen is not hope; for why does one still hope for what he sees? But if we hope for what we do not see, we eagerly wait for it with perseverance.

—ROMANS 8:18–19, 24–25

Through the LORD's mercies we are not consumed,
   Because His compassions fail not.
   They are new every morning;
   Great is Your faithfulness.
   "The LORD is my portion," says my soul,
   "Therefore I hope in Him!"

—LAMENTATIONS 3:22–24

With Guidance

A father becomes wise when he seeks the Lord for knowledge, understanding, and wisdom. Proverbs 3:13–15 says, "Happy is the man who finds wisdom, and the man who gains understanding; for her proceeds are better than the profits of silver, and her gain than fine gold. She is more precious than rubies, and all the things you may desire cannot compare with her." Guidance comes from the Lord through His Spirit. Read the Word of God often, asking the Spirit to lead you in all truth. The Scriptures will guide you, protect you, and give you all the wisdom you need to be the father God has called you to be.

Thus says the LORD, your Redeemer,
 The Holy One of Israel:
 "I am the LORD your God,
 Who teaches you to profit,
 Who leads you by the way you should go."

—ISAIAH 48:17

"The LORD will guide you continually,
 And satisfy your soul in drought,
 And strengthen your bones;
 You shall be like a watered garden,
 And like a spring of water, whose waters do
  not fail."

—ISAIAH 58:11

Trust in the LORD with all your heart,
 And lean not on your own understanding;
 In all your ways acknowledge Him,
 And He shall direct your paths.

—PROVERBS 3:5–6

GOD'S DYNAMIC
EXAMPLE OF FATHERS

Abraham

Now the LORD had said to Abram:

> *"Get out of your country,*
> *From your family*
> *And from your father's house,*
> *To a land that I will show you.*
> *I will make you a great nation;*
> *I will bless you*
> *And make your name great;*
> *And you shall be a blessing.*
> *I will bless those who bless you,*
> *And I will curse him who curses you;*
> *And in you all the families of the earth shall be*
> *blessed."*

—GENESIS 12:1–3

*When Abram was ninety-nine years old, the L*ORD
*appeared to Abram and said to him, "I am Almighty
God; walk before Me and be blameless. And I will
make My covenant between Me and you, and will
multiply you exceedingly." Then Abram fell on his face,
and God talked with him, saying: "As for Me, behold,
My covenant is with you, and you shall be a father of
many nations. No longer shall your name be called
Abram, but your name shall be Abraham; for I have
made you a father of many nations."*

—GENESIS 17:1–5

*And the L*ORD *visited Sarah as He had said, and the
L*ORD *did for Sarah as He had spoken. For Sarah conceived and bore Abraham a son in his old age, at the set
time of which God had spoken to him. And Abraham
called the name of his son who was born to him—
whom Sarah bore to him—Isaac. Then Abraham
circumcised his son Isaac when he was eight days old,
as God had commanded him. Now Abraham was one
hundred years old when his son Isaac was born to him.*

—GENESIS 21:1–5

Jacob

Then Jacob was left alone; and a Man wrestled with him until the breaking of day. Now when He saw that He did not prevail against him, He touched the socket of his hip; and the socket of Jacob's hip was out of joint as He wrestled with him. And He said, "Let Me go, for the day breaks." But he said, "I will not let You go unless You bless me!" So He said to him, "What is your name?" He said, "Jacob." And He said, "Your name shall no longer be called Jacob, but Israel; for you have struggled with God and with men, and have prevailed." Then Jacob asked, saying, "Tell me Your name, I pray." And He said, "Why is it that you ask about My name?" And He blessed him there. So Jacob called the name of the place Peniel: "For I have seen God face to face, and my life is preserved."

—GENESIS 32:24–30

Then God said to Jacob, "Arise, go up to Bethel and dwell there; and make an altar there to God, who appeared to you when you fled from the face of Esau your brother." And Jacob said to his household and to all who were with him, "Put away the foreign gods that are among you, purify yourselves, and change your garments. Then let us arise and go up to Bethel; and I will make an altar there to God, who answered me in the day of my distress and has been with me in the way which I have gone." So they gave Jacob all the foreign gods which were in their hands, and the earrings which were in their ears; and Jacob hid them under the terebinth tree which was by Shechem. And they journeyed, and the terror of God was upon the cities that were all around them, and they did not pursue the sons of Jacob.

—GENESIS 35:1–5

Joseph

*And to Joseph were born two sons before the years
of famine came, whom Asenath, the daughter of
Poti-Pherah priest of On, bore to him. Joseph called
the name of the firstborn Manasseh: "For God has
made me forget all my toil and all my father's house."
And the name of the second he called Ephraim: "For
God has caused me to be fruitful in the land of my
affliction." Then the seven years of plenty which were
in the land of Egypt ended, and the seven years of
famine began to come, as Joseph had said. The famine
was in all lands, but in all the land of Egypt there was
bread. So when all the land of Egypt was famished,
the people cried to Pharaoh for bread. Then Pharaoh
said to all the Egyptians, "Go to Joseph; whatever he
says to you, do." The famine was over all the face of
the earth, and Joseph opened all the storehouses and
sold to the Egyptians. And the famine became severe
in the land of Egypt. So all countries came to Joseph*

in Egypt to buy grain, because the famine was severe in all lands.

—Genesis 41:50–57

Then Joseph said to his brothers, "I am Joseph; does my father still live?" But his brothers could not answer him, for they were dismayed in his presence. And Joseph said to his brothers, "Please come near to me." So they came near. Then he said: "I am Joseph your brother, whom you sold into Egypt. But now, do not therefore be grieved or angry with yourselves because you sold me here; for God sent me before you to preserve life. For these two years the famine has been in the land, and there are still five years in which there will be neither plowing nor harvesting. And God sent me before you to preserve a posterity for you in the earth, and to save your lives by a great deliverance. So now it was not you who sent me here, but God; and He has made me a father to Pharaoh, and lord of all his house, and a ruler throughout all the land of Egypt."

—Genesis 45:3–8

David

Arise, O LORD, to Your resting place,
    You and the ark of Your strength.
    Let Your priests be clothed with righteousness,
    And let Your saints shout for joy.
    For Your servant David's sake,
    Do not turn away the face of Your Anointed.
    The LORD has sworn in truth to David;
    He will not turn from it:
    "I will set upon your throne the fruit of your body.
    If your sons will keep My covenant
    And My testimony which I shall teach them,
    Their sons also shall sit upon your throne
        forevermore."
    For the LORD has chosen Zion;
    He has desired it for His dwelling place:
    "This is My resting place forever;
    Here I will dwell, for I have desired it.

I will abundantly bless her provision;
I will satisfy her poor with bread.
I will also clothe her priests with salvation,
And her saints shall shout aloud for joy.
There I will make the horn of David grow;
I will prepare a lamp for My Anointed.
His enemies I will clothe with shame,
But upon Himself His crown shall flourish."

—PSALM 132:8–18

Then David spoke to the LORD the words of this song,
on the day when the LORD had delivered him from
the hand of all his enemies, and from the hand of
Saul. And he said:

"The LORD is my rock and my fortress and my
    deliverer. . . .
For You are my lamp, O LORD;
The LORD shall enlighten my darkness.
For by You I can run against a troop;
By my God I can leap over a wall."

—2 SAMUEL 22:1–2, 29–30

Manoah

Again the children of Israel did evil in the sight of the LORD, and the LORD delivered them into the hand of the Philistines for forty years. Now there was a certain man from Zorah, of the family of the Danites, whose name was Manoah; and his wife was barren and had no children. And the Angel of the LORD appeared to the woman and said to her, "Indeed now, you are barren and have borne no children, but you shall conceive and bear a son. Now therefore, please be careful not to drink wine or similar drink, and not to eat anything unclean. For behold, you shall conceive and bear a son. And no razor shall come upon his head, for the child shall be a Nazirite to God from the womb; and he shall begin to deliver Israel out of the hand of the Philistines." So the woman came and told her husband, saying, "A Man of God came to me, and His countenance was like the countenance of the

Angel of God, very awesome; but I did not ask Him where He was from, and He did not tell me His name. And He said to me, 'Behold, you shall conceive and bear a son. Now drink no wine or similar drink, nor eat anything unclean, for the child shall be a Nazirite to God from the womb to the day of his death.'" . . . *So the woman bore a son and called his name Samson; and the child grew, and the Lord blessed him. And the Spirit of the LORD began to move upon him at Mahaneh Dan between Zorah and Eshtaol.*

—JUDGES 13:1–7, 24–25

Zacharias

There was in the days of Herod, the king of Judea, a certain priest named Zacharias, of the division of Abijah. His wife was of the daughters of Aaron, and her name was Elizabeth. And they were both right- eous before God, walking in all the commandments and ordinances of the Lord blameless. But they had no child, because Elizabeth was barren, and they were both well advanced in years. So it was, that while he was serving as priest before God in the order of his division . . . an angel of the Lord appeared to him, standing on the right side of the altar of incense. And when Zacharias saw him, he was troubled, and fear fell upon him. But the angel said to him, "Do not be afraid, Zacharias, for your prayer is heard; and your wife Elizabeth will bear you a son, and you shall call his name John. And you will have joy and gladness, and many will rejoice at his birth. For he will be

great in the sight of the Lord, and shall drink neither wine nor strong drink. He will also be filled with the Holy Spirit, even from his mother's womb. . . . Now Elizabeth's full time came for her to be delivered, and she brought forth a son. When her neighbors and relatives heard how the Lord had shown great mercy to her, they rejoiced with her. So it was, on the eighth day, that they came to circumcise the child; and they would have called him by the name of his father, Zacharias. His mother answered and said, "No; he shall be called John." But they said to her, "There is no one among your relatives who is called by this name." So they made signs to his father—what he would have him called. And he asked for a writing tablet, and wrote, saying, "His name is John." So they all marveled. Immediately his mouth was opened and his tongue loosed, and he spoke, praising God. . . .

"Blessed is the Lord God of Israel,
For He has visited and redeemed His people."
—Luke 1:5–8, 11–15, 57–64, 68

Noah

And he called his name Noah, saying, "This one will comfort us concerning our work and the toil of our hands, because of the ground which the Lord has cursed."

—Genesis 5:29

So the Lord said, "I will destroy man whom I have created from the face of the earth, both man and beast, creeping thing and birds of the air, for I am sorry that I have made them." But Noah found grace in the eyes of the Lord. This is the genealogy of Noah. Noah was a just man, perfect in his generations. Noah walked with God. And Noah begot three sons: Shem, Ham, and Japheth.

—Genesis 6:7–10

So He destroyed all living things which were on the face of the ground: both man and cattle, creeping thing and bird of the air. They were destroyed from the earth. Only Noah and those who were with him in the ark remained alive. And the waters prevailed on the earth one hundred and fifty days. Then God remembered Noah, and every living thing, and all the animals that were with him in the ark. And God made a wind to pass over the earth, and the waters subsided.

—GENESIS 7:23—8:1

So God blessed Noah and his sons, and said to them: "Be fruitful and multiply, and fill the earth." . . . Then God spoke to Noah and to his sons with him, saying: "And as for Me, behold, I establish My covenant with you and with your descendants after you."

—GENESIS 9:1, 8—9

Joseph

Now the birth of Jesus Christ was as follows: After His mother Mary was betrothed to Joseph, before they came together, she was found with child of the Holy Spirit. Then Joseph her husband, being a just man, and not wanting to make her a public example, was minded to put her away secretly. But while he thought about these things, behold, an angel of the Lord appeared to him in a dream, saying, "Joseph, son of David, do not be afraid to take to you Mary your wife, for that which is conceived in her is of the Holy Spirit. And she will bring forth a Son, and you shall call His name JESUS, for He will save His people from their sins." So all this was done that it might be fulfilled which was spoken by the Lord through the prophet, saying: "Behold, the virgin shall be with child, and bear a Son, and they shall call His name Immanuel," which is translated, "God with us." Then

Joseph, being aroused from sleep, did as the angel of the Lord commanded him and took to him his wife, and did not know her till she had brought forth her firstborn Son. And he called His name JESUS.

—MATTHEW 1:18–25

Now when they had departed, behold, an angel of the Lord appeared to Joseph in a dream, saying, "Arise, take the young Child and His mother, flee to Egypt, and stay there until I bring you word; for Herod will seek the young Child to destroy Him." When he arose, he took the young Child and His mother by night and departed for Egypt . . . . Now when Herod was dead, behold, an angel of the Lord appeared in a dream to Joseph in Egypt, saying, "Arise, take the young Child and His mother, and go to the land of Israel, for those who sought the young Child's life are dead." Then he arose, took the young Child and His mother, and came into the land of Israel.

—MATTHEW 2:13–14, 19–21

SCRIPTURE
MEDITATIONS
FOR FATHERS

Meditations of Faith

Many are they who say of me,
    "There is no help for him in God."
    But You, O Lord, are a shield for me,
    My glory and the One who lifts up my head.
    I cried to the Lord with my voice,
    And He heard me from His holy hill.
    I lay down and slept;
    I awoke, for the Lord sustained me.
    I will not be afraid of ten thousands of people
    Who have set themselves against me all around.
    Arise, O Lord;
    Save me, O my God!
    For You have struck all my enemies on the
        cheekbone;
    You have broken the teeth of the ungodly.
    Salvation belongs to the Lord.
    Your blessing is upon Your people.

                                    —Psalm 3:2–8

Be anxious for nothing, but in everything by prayer and supplication, with thanksgiving, let your requests be made known to God; and the peace of God, which surpasses all understanding, will guard your hearts and minds through Christ Jesus.

—Philippians 4:6–7

Therefore, having been justified by faith, we have peace with God through our Lord Jesus Christ, through whom also we have access by faith into this grace in which we stand, and rejoice in hope of the glory of God. And not only that, but we also glory in tribulations, knowing that tribulation produces perseverance; and perseverance, character; and character, hope. Now hope does not disappoint, because the love of God has been poured out in our hearts by the Holy Spirit who was given to us.

—Romans 5:1–5

Therefore we also, since we are surrounded by so great a cloud of witnesses, let us lay aside every weight, and the sin which so easily ensnares us, and let us run with endurance the race that is set before us, looking unto Jesus, the author and finisher of our faith, who for the joy that was set before Him endured the cross, despising the shame, and has sat down at the right hand of the throne of God.

—HEBREWS 12:1–2

My soul, wait silently for God alone,
    For my expectation is from Him.
    He only is my rock and my salvation;
    He is my defense;
    I shall not be moved.
    In God is my salvation and my glory;
    The rock of my strength,
    And my refuge, is in God.
    Trust in Him at all times, you people;
    Pour out your heart before Him;
    God is a refuge for us.

—PSALM 62:5–8

God is our refuge and strength,
A very present help in trouble.
Therefore we will not fear,
Even though the earth be removed,
And though the mountains be carried into the
midst of the sea;
Though its waters roar and be troubled,
Though the mountains shake with its swelling.
There is a river whose streams shall make glad
the city of God,
The holy place of the tabernacle of the Most
High.

—Psalm 46:1–4

But you, beloved, building yourselves up on your most holy faith, praying in the Holy Spirit, keep yourselves in the love of God, looking for the mercy of our Lord Jesus Christ unto eternal life.

—Jude vv. 20–21

Meditations for Hope

Through the LORD's mercies we are not consumed,
    Because His compassions fail not.
    They are new every morning;
    Great is Your faithfulness.
    "The LORD is my portion," says my soul,
    "Therefore I hope in Him!"
    The LORD is good to those who wait for Him,
    To the soul who seeks Him.

                          —LAMENTATIONS 3:22–25

I would have lost heart, unless I had believed
    That I would see the goodness of the LORD
    In the land of the living.
    Wait on the LORD;
    Be of good courage,
    And He shall strengthen your heart;
    Wait, I say, on the LORD!

                          —PSALM 27:13–14

"Hear, O Lord, and have mercy on me;
  Lord, be my helper!"
  You have turned for me my mourning into
    dancing;
  You have put off my sackcloth and clothed me
    with gladness.

—Psalm 30:10–11

We are hard-pressed on every side, yet not crushed;
we are perplexed, but not in despair; persecuted, but
not forsaken; struck down, but not destroyed—always
carrying about in the body the dying of the Lord Jesus,
that the life of Jesus also may be manifested in our
body. For we who live are always delivered to death for
Jesus' sake, that the life of Jesus also may be manifested
in our mortal flesh. So then death is working in us, but
life in you.

—2 Corinthians 4:8–12

Who shall separate us from the love of Christ? Shall tribulation, or distress, or persecution, or famine, or nakedness, or peril, or sword? As it is written:

"For Your sake we are killed all day long;
*   We are accounted as sheep for the slaughter."*

Yet in all these things we are more than conquerors through Him who loved us. For I am persuaded that neither death nor life, nor angels nor principalities nor powers, nor things present nor things to come, nor height nor depth, nor any other created thing, shall be able to separate us from the love of God which is in Christ Jesus our Lord.

—ROMANS 8:35–39

"Come to Me, all you who labor and are heavy laden, and I will give you rest. Take My yoke upon you and learn from Me, for I am gentle and lowly in heart, and you will find rest for your souls. For My yoke is easy and My burden is light."

—MATTHEW 11:28–30

Therefore do not cast away your confidence, which has great reward. For you have need of endurance, so that after you have done the will of God, you may receive the promise:

"For yet a little while,
>   And He who is coming will come and will not
>   tarry.
>   Now the just shall live by faith;
>   But if anyone draws back,
>   My soul has no pleasure in him."

—HEBREWS 10:35–38

For our light affliction, which is but for a moment, is working for us a far more exceeding and eternal weight of glory, while we do not look at the things which are seen, but at the things which are not seen. For the things which are seen are temporary, but the things which are not seen are eternal.

—2 CORINTHIANS 4:17–18

Meditations for Peace

"All your children shall be taught by the LORD,
    And great shall be the peace of your children.
    In righteousness you shall be established;
    You shall be far from oppression, for you shall
        not fear;
    And from terror, for it shall not come near you.
    Indeed they shall surely assemble, but not
        because of Me.
    Whoever assembles against you shall fall for
        your sake."

—ISAIAH 54:13–15

I will hear what God the LORD will speak,
    For He will speak peace
    To His people and to His saints.

—PSALM 85:8

"The LORD will guide you continually,
    And satisfy your soul in drought,
    And strengthen your bones;
    You shall be like a watered garden,
    And like a spring of water, whose waters do
        not fail."

—ISAIAH 58:11

Let the words of my mouth and the meditation of my
heart
    Be acceptable in Your sight,
    O LORD, my strength and my Redeemer.

—PSALM 19:14

Be anxious for nothing, but in everything by prayer
and supplication, with thanksgiving, let your requests
be made known to God; and the peace of God, which
surpasses all understanding, will guard your hearts
and minds through Christ Jesus.

—PHILIPPIANS 4:6–7

Meditations on the Power of God

"I am He who lives, and was dead, and behold, I
am alive forevermore. Amen. And I have the keys of
Hades and of Death."

—REVELATION 1:18

"But hold fast what you have till I come. And he who
overcomes, and keeps My works until the end, to him I
will give power over the nations—'He shall rule them
with a rod of iron; they shall be dashed to pieces like
the potter's vessels'—as I also have received from My
Father; and I will give him the morning star."

—REVELATION 2:25–28

Now I saw a new heaven and a new earth, for the first
heaven and the first earth had passed away. Also there
was no more sea. Then I, John, saw the holy city, New
Jerusalem, coming down out of heaven from God, prepared as a bride adorned for her husband. And I heard

a loud voice from heaven saying, "Behold, the tabernacle of God is with men, and He will dwell with them, and they shall be His people. God Himself will be with them and be their God. And God will wipe away every tear from their eyes; there shall be no more death, nor sorrow, nor crying. There shall be no more pain, for the former things have passed away." Then He who sat on the throne said, "Behold, I make all things new." And He said to me, "Write, for these words are true and faithful." And He said to me, "It is done! I am the Alpha and the Omega, the Beginning and the End. I will give of the fountain of the water of life freely to him who thirsts. He who overcomes shall inherit all things, and I will be his God and he shall be My son."

—REVELATION 21:1–7

Meditations of Praise

My heart is steadfast, O God, my heart is steadfast;
I will sing and give praise.
Awake, my glory!
Awake, lute and harp!
I will awaken the dawn.
I will praise You, O Lord, among the peoples;
I will sing to You among the nations.

—PSALM 57:7–9

Oh, give thanks to the LORD, for He is good!
For His mercy endures forever.
Oh, give thanks to the God of gods!
For His mercy endures forever.
Oh, give thanks to the Lord of lords!
For His mercy endures forever: . . .
Oh, give thanks to the God of heaven!
For His mercy endures forever.

—PSALM 136:1–3, 26

Let the saints be joyful in glory;
Let them sing aloud on their beds.
Let the high praises of God be in their mouth,
And a two-edged sword in their hand.

—Psalm 149:5–6

Praise the Lord!
Praise God in His sanctuary;
Praise Him in His mighty firmament!
Praise Him for His mighty acts;
Praise Him according to His excellent greatness!
Praise Him with the sound of the trumpet;
Praise Him with the lute and harp!
Praise Him with the timbrel and dance;
Praise Him with stringed instruments and flutes!
Praise Him with loud cymbals;
Praise Him with clashing cymbals!
Let everything that has breath praise the Lord.
Praise the Lord!

—Psalm 150

Meditations for Trust

Those who trust in the LORD
Are like Mount Zion,
Which cannot be moved, but abides forever.
As the mountains surround Jerusalem,
So the LORD surrounds His people
From this time forth and forever.
For the scepter of wickedness shall not rest
On the land allotted to the righteous,
Lest the righteous reach out their hands to iniquity.
Do good, O LORD, to those who are good,
And to those who are upright in their hearts.

—PSALM 125:1–4

Trust in the LORD with all your heart,
And lean not on your own understanding;
In all your ways acknowledge Him,
And He shall direct your paths.

—PROVERBS 3:5–6

LORD, how they have increased who trouble me!
>   Many are they who rise up against me.
>   Many are they who say of me,
>   "There is no help for him in God."
>   But You, O LORD, are a shield for me,
>   My glory and the One who lifts up my head.
>   I cried to the LORD with my voice,
>   And He heard me from His holy hill.
>   I lay down and slept;
>   I awoke, for the LORD sustained me.
>   I will not be afraid of ten thousands of people
>   Who have set themselves against me all around.
>   Arise, O LORD;
>   Save me, O my God!
>   For You have struck all my enemies on the
>   cheekbone
>   You have broken the teeth of the ungodly.
>   Salvation belongs to the LORD.
>   Your blessing is upon Your people.
>   —PSALM 3:1–8

Meditations for Victory

*To You, O L*ORD*, I lift up my soul.*
O my God, I trust in You;
Let me not be ashamed;
Let not my enemies triumph over me.
*—P*SALM *25:1–2*

*The righteous cry out, and the L*ORD *hears,*
And delivers them out of all their troubles.
*The L*ORD *is near to those who have a broken*
heart,
And saves such as have a contrite spirit.
Many are the afflictions of the righteous,
*But the L*ORD *delivers him out of them all.*
*—P*SALM *34:17–19*

"Have I not commanded you? Be strong and of good
courage; do not be afraid, nor be dismayed, for the
*L*ORD *your God is with you wherever you go."*
*—J*OSHUA *1:9*

Blessed is he who considers the poor;
The LORD will deliver him in time of trouble.
The LORD will preserve him and keep him alive,
And he will be blessed on the earth;
You will not deliver him to the will of his
enemies.
The LORD will strengthen him on his bed of
illness;
You will sustain him on his sickbed.

—PSALM 41:1–3

In this you greatly rejoice . . . that the genuineness
of your faith, being much more precious than gold
that perishes, though it is tested by fire, may be found
to praise, honor, and glory at the revelation of Jesus
Christ, whom having not seen you love. Though now
you do not see Him, yet believing, you rejoice with
joy inexpressible and full of glory, receiving the end of
your faith—the salvation of your souls.

—1 PETER 1:6–9

SCRIPTURE MEDITATIONS FOR FATHERS

Meditations for Joy

*My brethren, count it all joy when you fall into
various trials, knowing that the testing of your faith
produces patience. But let patience have its perfect
work, that you may be perfect and complete, lacking
nothing.*

—James 1:2–4

Let them shout for joy and be glad,
    Who favor my righteous cause;
    And let them say continually,
    "Let the Lord be magnified,*
    Who has pleasure in the prosperity of His
        servant."
    And my tongue shall speak of Your righteousness
    And of Your praise all the day long.

—Psalm 35:27–28

Blessed are the people who know the joyful sound!
  They walk, O LORD, in the light of Your
    countenance.
  In Your name they rejoice all day long,
  And in Your righteousness they are exalted.
  For You are the glory of their strength,
  And in Your favor our horn is exalted.
                                        —PSALM 89:15–17

For His anger is but for a moment,
  His favor is for life;
  Weeping may endure for a night,
  But joy comes in the morning.
                                        —PSALM 30:5

Make a joyful shout to the LORD, all you lands!
  Serve the LORD with gladness;
  Come before His presence with singing.
  Know that the LORD, He is God;
  It is He who has made us, and not we ourselves;
  We are His people and the sheep of His pasture.
                                        —PSALM 100:1–3

Meditations of Grace

And He said to me, "My grace is sufficient for you, for My strength is made perfect in weakness." Therefore most gladly I will rather boast in my infirmities, that the power of Christ may rest upon me.

—2 CORINTHIANS 12:9

You are fairer than the sons of men;
> *Grace is poured upon Your lips;*
> *Therefore God has blessed You forever.*
> *Gird Your sword upon Your thigh, O Mighty One,*
> *With Your glory and Your majesty.*
> *And in Your majesty ride prosperously because of*
> > *truth, humility, and righteousness;*
> *And Your right hand shall teach You awesome*
> > *things.*

—PSALM 45:2–4

*For by grace you have been saved through faith,
and that not of yourselves; it is the gift of God, not
of works, lest anyone should boast. For we are His
workmanship, created in Christ Jesus for good works,
which God prepared beforehand that we should walk
in them.*

—Ephesians 2:8–10

*For the Lord God is a sun and shield;
    The Lord will give grace and glory;
    No good thing will He withhold
    From those who walk uprightly.*

—Psalm 84:11

*He who loves purity of heart
    And has grace on his lips,
    The king will be his friend.*

—Proverbs 22:11

Meditations for Mercy

Oh, give thanks to the Lord, for He is good!
    For His mercy endures forever.
    And say, "Save us, O God of our salvation;
    Gather us together, and deliver us from the
        Gentiles,
    To give thanks to Your holy name,
    To triumph in Your praise."
    Blessed be the Lord God of Israel
    From everlasting to everlasting!

And all the people said, "Amen!" and praised
the Lord.

—1 CHRONICLES 16:34–36

But I have trusted in Your mercy;
My heart shall rejoice in Your salvation.
I will sing to the LORD,
Because He has dealt bountifully with me.

—Psalm 13:5–6

"O Lord, I pray, please let Your ear be attentive to
the prayer of Your servant, and to the prayer of Your
servants who desire to fear Your name; and let Your
servant prosper this day, I pray, and grant him mercy
in the sight of this man."

For I was the king's cupbearer.

—Nehemiah 1:11

But as for me, I will come into Your house in the mul-
titude of Your mercy;
In fear of You I will worship toward Your holy
temple.
Lead me, O LORD, in Your righteousness because
of my enemies;
Make Your way straight before my face.

—Psalm 5:7–8

Meditations in God's Love

I will extol You, my God, O King;
    And I will bless Your name forever and ever.
    Every day I will bless You,
    And I will praise Your name forever and ever.
    Great is the LORD, and greatly to be praised;
    And His greatness is unsearchable.
    One generation shall praise Your works to
        another,
    And shall declare Your mighty acts.
    I will meditate on the glorious splendor of Your
        majesty,
    And on Your wondrous works.

                                    —PSALM 145:1–5

Who shall separate us from the love of Christ? Shall tribulation, or distress, or persecution, or famine, or nakedness, or peril, or sword? As it is written:

"For Your sake we are killed all day long;
　We are accounted as sheep for the slaughter."

Yet in all these things we are more than conquerors through Him who loved us. For I am persuaded that neither death nor life, nor angels nor principalities nor powers, nor things present nor things to come, nor height nor depth, nor any other created thing, shall be able to separate us from the love of God which is in Christ Jesus our Lord.

—ROMANS 8:35–39

He who does not love does not know God, for God is love. In this the love of God was manifested toward us, that God has sent His only begotten Son into the world, that we might live through Him. In this is love, not that we loved God, but that He loved us and sent His Son to be the propitiation for our sins. Beloved, if God so loved us, we also ought to love one another.

—1 JOHN 4:8–11

Meditations for God's Promises

Hear my cry, O God;
Attend to my prayer.
From the end of the earth I will cry to You,
When my heart is overwhelmed;
Lead me to the rock that is higher than I.
For You have been a shelter for me,
A strong tower from the enemy.
I will abide in Your tabernacle forever;
I will trust in the shelter of Your wings.

—PSALM 61:1–4

Then I proclaimed a fast there at the river of Ahava,
that we might humble ourselves before our God, to
seek from Him the right way for us and our little ones
and all our possessions. For I was ashamed to request
of the king an escort of soldiers and horsemen to help
us against the enemy on the road, because we had

*spoken to the king, saying, "The hand of our God is
upon all those for good who seek Him, but His power
and His wrath are against all those who forsake Him."
So we fasted and entreated our God for this, and He
answered our prayer.*

—EZRA 8:21–23

*He who dwells in the secret place of the Most High
    Shall abide under the shadow of the Almighty.
I will say of the LORD, "He is my refuge and my
        fortress;
My God, in Him I will trust."
Surely He shall deliver you from the snare of the
        fowler
And from the perilous pestilence.
He shall cover you with His feathers,
And under His wings you shall take refuge;
His truth shall be your shield and buckler.*

—PSALM 91:1–4

CRISIS SCRIPTURE
GUIDE

Addiction

Stand fast therefore in the liberty by which Christ has made us free, and do not be entangled again with a yoke of bondage.

—GALATIANS 5:1

"And you shall know the truth, and the truth shall make you free."

—JOHN 8:32

Wine is a mocker,
    Strong drink is a brawler,
    And whoever is led astray by it is not wise.

—PROVERBS 20:1

Aging

For by me your days will be multiplied,
And years of life will be added to you.

—PROVERBS 9:11

Therefore remove sorrow from your heart,
And put away evil from your flesh,
For childhood and youth are vanity.

—ECCLESIASTES 11:10

The fear of the LORD prolongs days,
But the years of the wicked will be shortened.

—PROVERBS 10:27

CRISIS SCRIPTURE GUIDE
Anger

Who, when He was reviled, did not revile in return; when He suffered, He did not threaten, but committed Himself to Him who judges righteously.

—1 PETER 2:23

"Be angry, and do not sin": do not let the sun go down on your wrath, nor give place to the devil.

—EPHESIANS 4:26–27

For God did not appoint us to wrath, but to obtain salvation through our Lord Jesus Christ.

—1 THESSALONIANS 5:9

CRISIS SCRIPTURE GUIDE
Anxiety

"Peace I leave with you, My peace I give to you; not as the world gives do I give to you. Let not your heart be troubled, neither let it be afraid."

—JOHN 14:27

Be anxious for nothing, but in everything by prayer and supplication, with thanksgiving, let your requests be made known to God; and the peace of God, which surpasses all understanding, will guard your hearts and minds through Christ Jesus. Finally, brethren, whatever things are true, whatever things are noble, whatever things are just, whatever things are pure, whatever things are lovely, whatever things are of good report, if there is any virtue and if there is anything praiseworthy—meditate on these things.

—PHILIPPIANS 4:6–8

CRISIS SCRIPTURE GUIDE
Backsliding

He who covers his sins will not prosper,
But whoever confesses and forsakes them will
have mercy.

—PROVERBS 28:13

Create in me a clean heart, O God,
And renew a steadfast spirit within me.
Do not cast me away from Your presence,
And do not take Your Holy Spirit from me.
Restore to me the joy of Your salvation,
And uphold me by Your generous Spirit.

—PSALM 51:10–12

"All that the Father gives Me will come to Me, and the
one who comes to Me I will by no means cast out."

—JOHN 6:37

CRISIS SCRIPTURE GUIDE

Bereavement

So when this corruptible has put on incorruption,
and this mortal has put on immortality, then shall be
brought to pass the saying that is written: "Death is
swallowed up in victory."

"O Death, where is your sting?
O Hades, where is your victory?"

The sting of death is sin, and the strength of sin
is the law. But thanks be to God, who gives us the
victory through our Lord Jesus Christ.

—1 CORINTHIANS 15:54–57

He will swallow up death forever,
And the Lord GOD will wipe away tears from
all faces;
The rebuke of His people
He will take away from all the earth;
For the LORD has spoken.

—ISAIAH 25:8

CRISIS SCRIPTURE GUIDE
Bitterness

Let all bitterness, wrath, anger, clamor, and evil speaking be put away from you, with all malice.
—Ephesians 4:31

Looking carefully lest anyone fall short of the grace of God; lest any root of bitterness springing up cause trouble, and by this many become defiled.
—Hebrews 12:15

But if you have bitter envy and self-seeking in your hearts, do not boast and lie against the truth. This wisdom does not descend from above, but is earthly, sensual, demonic.

—James 3:14–15

CRISIS SCRIPTURE GUIDE

Carnality

Knowing this, that our old man was crucified with Him, that the body of sin might be done away with, that we should no longer be slaves of sin. For he who has died has been freed from sin. Now if we died with Christ, we believe that we shall also live with Him, knowing that Christ, having been raised from the dead, dies no more. Death no longer has dominion over Him.

—ROMANS 6:6–9

That you put off, concerning your former conduct, the old man which grows corrupt according to the deceitful lusts, and be renewed in the spirit of your mind, and that you put on the new man which was created according to God, in true righteousness and holiness.

—EPHESIANS 4:22–24

Condemnation

There is therefore now no condemnation to those who are in Christ Jesus, who do not walk according to the flesh, but according to the Spirit.

—ROMANS 8:1

As it is written:

> *"There is none righteous, no, not one;*
> *There is none who understands;*
> *There is none who seeks after God.*
> *They have all turned aside;*
> *They have together become unprofitable;*
> *There is none who does good, no, not one."*

—ROMANS 3:10–12

CRISIS SCRIPTURE GUIDE
Confession

You will keep him in perfect peace,
Whose mind is stayed on You,
Because he trusts in You.

—ISAIAH 26:3

For God is not the author of confusion but of peace, as in all the churches of the saints.

—1 CORINTHIANS 14:33

"For My thoughts are not your thoughts,
Nor are your ways My ways," says the LORD.
"For as the heavens are higher than the earth,
So are My ways higher than your ways,
And My thoughts than your thoughts."

—ISAIAH 55:8–9

Death

For none of us lives to himself, and no one dies to himself. For if we live, we live to the Lord; and if we die, we die to the Lord. Therefore, whether we live or die, we are the Lord's.

—Romans 14:7–8

For I know that my Redeemer lives,
   And He shall stand at last on the earth;
   And after my skin is destroyed, this I know,
   That in my flesh I shall see God,
   Whom I shall see for myself,
   And my eyes shall behold, and not another.
   How my heart yearns within me!

—Job 19:25–27

Depression

Then he said to them, "Go your way, eat the fat, drink the sweet, and send portions to those for whom nothing is prepared; for this day is holy to our Lord. Do not sorrow, for the joy of the LORD is your strength."

—NEHEMIAH 8:10

Finally, brethren, whatever things are true, whatever things are noble, whatever things are just, whatever things are pure, whatever things are lovely, whatever things are of good report, if there is any virtue and if there is anything praiseworthy—meditate on these things.

—PHILIPPIANS 4:8

And we know that all things work together for good to those who love God, to those who are the called according to His purpose.

—ROMANS 8:28

Dissatisfaction

Hell and Destruction are never full;
    So the eyes of man are never satisfied.

           —Proverbs 27:20

Let your conduct be without covetousness; be content with such things as you have. For He Himself has said, "I will never leave you nor forsake you." So we may boldly say:

    "The Lord is my helper;
    I will not fear.
    What can man do to me?"

           —Hebrews 13:5–6

Now godliness with contentment is great gain. For we brought nothing into this world, and it is certain we can carry nothing out. And having food and clothing, with these we shall be content.

           —1 Timothy 6:6–8

Doubt

So then faith comes by hearing, and hearing by the word of God.

—Romans 10:17

But recall the former days in which, after you were illuminated, you endured a great struggle with sufferings . . . . Therefore do not cast away your confidence, which has great reward. For you have need of endurance, so that after you have done the will of God, you may receive the promise:

"For yet a little while,
And He who is coming will come and will not tarry.
Now the just shall live by faith;
But if anyone draws back,
My soul has no pleasure in him."

But we are not of those who draw back to perdition, but of those who believe to the saving of the soul.

—Hebrews 10:32, 35–39

Failure

For a righteous man may fall seven times
>   And rise again,
>   But the wicked shall fall by calamity.
>   Do not rejoice when your enemy falls,
>   And do not let your heart be glad when he
>   stumbles;
>   Lest the LORD see it, and it displease Him,
>   And He turn away His wrath from him.

—PROVERBS 24:16–18

The LORD upholds all who fall,
>   And raises up all who are bowed down.
>   The eyes of all look expectantly to You,
>   And You give them their food in due season.
>   You open Your hand
>   And satisfy the desire of every living thing.

—PSALM 145:14–16

Fear

For God has not given us a spirit of fear, but of power and of love and of a sound mind.

—2 TIMOTHY 1:7

I can do all things through Christ who strengthens me.

—PHILIPPIANS 4:13

And when I saw Him, I fell at His feet as dead. But He laid His right hand on me, saying to me, "Do not be afraid; I am the First and the Last. I am He who lives, and was dead, and behold, I am alive forevermore. Amen. And I have the keys of Hades and of Death."

—REVELATION 1:17–18

Finances

"Therefore do not worry, saying, 'What shall we eat?' or 'What shall we drink?' or 'What shall we wear?' For after all these things the Gentiles seek. For your heavenly Father knows that you need all these things. But seek first the kingdom of God and His righteousness, and all these things shall be added to you. Therefore do not worry about tomorrow, for tomorrow will worry about its own things. Sufficient for the day is its own trouble."

—MATTHEW 6:31–34

I have been young, and now am old;
    Yet I have not seen the righteous forsaken,
    Nor his descendants begging bread.
    He is ever merciful, and lends;
    And his descendants are blessed.

—PSALM 37:25–26

CRISIS SCRIPTURE GUIDE
Illness

Is anyone among you sick? Let him call for the elders of the church, and let them pray over him, anointing him with oil in the name of the Lord.

—JAMES 5:14

He makes me to lie down in green pastures;
    He leads me beside the still waters.
    He restores my soul;
    He leads me in the paths of righteousness
    For His name's sake.
    Yea, though I walk through the valley of the
        shadow of death,
    I will fear no evil;
    For You are with me;
    Your rod and Your staff, they comfort me.

—PSALM 23:2–4

Insecurity

*But the Lord is faithful, who will establish you and
guard you from the evil one.*

—2 Thessalonians 3:3

Surely He shall deliver you from the snare of the fowler
 And from the perilous pestilence.
 He shall cover you with His feathers,
 And under His wings you shall take refuge;
 His truth shall be your shield and buckler.
 You shall not be afraid of the terror by night,
 Nor of the arrow that flies by day,
 Nor of the pestilence that walks in darkness,
 Nor of the destruction that lays waste at
 noonday.
 A thousand may fall at your side,
 And ten thousand at your right hand;
 But it shall not come near you.

—Psalm 91:3–7

Judging

Therefore judge nothing before the time, until the Lord comes, who will both bring to light the hidden things of darkness and reveal the counsels of the hearts. Then each one's praise will come from God.

—1 CORINTHIANS 4:5

"And why do you look at the speck in your brother's eye, but do not consider the plank in your own eye? Or how can you say to your brother, 'Let me remove the speck from your eye'; and look, a plank is in your own eye? Hypocrite! First remove the plank from your own eye, and then you will see clearly to remove the speck from your brother's eye."

—MATTHEW 7:3–5

"For the Father judges no one, but has committed all judgment to the Son."

—JOHN 5:22

Loneliness

"I will not leave you orphans; I will come to you."
—JOHN 14:18

He heals the brokenhearted
And binds up their wounds.
—PSALM 147:3

When my father and my mother forsake me,
Then the LORD will take care of me.
—PSALM 27:10

Lust

The Lord knows how to deliver the godly out of temptations and to reserve the unjust under punishment for the day of judgment.

—2 PETER 2:9

"If your eye causes you to sin, pluck it out and cast it from you. It is better for you to enter into life with one eye, rather than having two eyes, to be cast into hell fire."

—MATTHEW 18:9

Do not lust after her beauty in your heart,
 Nor let her allure you with her eyelids.
 For by means of a harlot
 A man is reduced to a crust of bread;
 And an adulteress will prey upon his precious life.

—PROVERBS 6:25–26

Marriage

Do not be unequally yoked together with unbelievers. For what fellowship has righteousness with lawlessness? And what communion has light with darkness? And what accord has Christ with Belial? Or what part has a believer with an unbeliever? And what agreement has the temple of God with idols? For you are the temple of the living God. As God has said:

> *"I will dwell in them*
> *And walk among them.*
> *I will be their God,*
> *And they shall be My people."*

Therefore

> *"Come out from among them*
> *And be separate, says the Lord.*
> *Do not touch what is unclean,*
> *And I will receive you."*

—2 Corinthians 6:14–17

Now to the married I command, yet not I but the Lord: A wife is not to depart from her husband. But even if she does depart, let her remain unmarried or be reconciled to her husband. And a husband is not to divorce his wife. But to the rest I, not the Lord, say: If any brother has a wife who does not believe, and she is willing to live with him, let him not divorce her. And a woman who has a husband who does not believe, if he is willing to live with her, let her not divorce him. For the unbelieving husband is sanctified by the wife, and the unbelieving wife is sanctified by the husband; otherwise your children would be unclean, but now they are holy. But if the unbeliever departs, let him depart; a brother or a sister is not under bondage in such cases. But God has called us to peace. For how do you know, O wife, whether you will save your husband? Or how do you know, O husband, whether you will save your wife? But as God has distributed to each one, as the Lord has called each one, so let him walk. And so I ordain in all the churches.

—1 Corinthians 7:10–17

Pride

Then Jesus called a little child to Him, set him in the midst of them, and said, "Assuredly, I say to you, unless you are converted and become as little children, you will by no means enter the kingdom of heaven. Therefore whoever humbles himself as this little child is the greatest in the kingdom of heaven."

—MATTHEW 18:2–4

Do not boast about tomorrow,
For you do not know what a day may bring forth.
Let another man praise you, and not your own
mouth;
A stranger, and not your own lips.

—PROVERBS 27:1–2

Satan

Finally, my brethren, be strong in the Lord and in the power of His might. Put on the whole armor of God, that you may be able to stand against the wiles of the devil. For we do not wrestle against flesh and blood, but against principalities, against powers, against the rulers of the darkness of this age, against spiritual hosts of wickedness in the heavenly places. Therefore take up the whole armor of God, that you may be able to withstand in the evil day, and having done all, to stand. Stand therefore, having girded your waist with truth, having put on the breastplate of righteousness, and having shod your feet with the preparation of the gospel of peace; above all, taking the shield of faith with which you will be able to quench all the fiery darts of the wicked one. And take the helmet of salvation, and the sword of the Spirit, which is the word of God.

—EPHESIANS 6:10–17

*Beloved, do not believe every spirit, but test the spirits,
whether they are of God; because many false prophets
have gone out into the world. By this you know the
Spirit of God: Every spirit that confesses that Jesus
Christ has come in the flesh is of God, and every spirit
that does not confess that Jesus Christ has come in the
flesh is not of God. And this is the spirit of the Anti-
christ, which you have heard was coming, and is now
already in the world.*

—1 JOHN 4:1–3

*And He said to them, "I saw Satan fall like lightning
from heaven. Behold, I give you the authority to
trample on serpents and scorpions, and over all the
power of the enemy, and nothing shall by any means
hurt you."*

—LUKE 10:18–19

Suffering

Though He was a Son, yet He learned obedience by the things which He suffered. And having been perfected, He became the author of eternal salvation to all who obey Him.

—HEBREWS 5:8–9

We are hard-pressed on every side, yet not crushed; we are perplexed, but not in despair; persecuted, but not forsaken; struck down, but not destroyed—always carrying about in the body the dying of the Lord Jesus, that the life of Jesus also may be manifested in our body.

—2 CORINTHIANS 4:8–10

Therefore let those who suffer according to the will of God commit their souls to Him in doing good, as to a faithful Creator.

—1 PETER 4:19

Temptation

Blessed is the man who endures temptation; for when he has been approved, he will receive the crown of life which the Lord has promised to those who love Him.

—JAMES 1:12

Beloved, do not think it strange concerning the fiery trial which is to try you, as though some strange thing happened to you; but rejoice to the extent that you partake of Christ's sufferings, that when His glory is revealed, you may also be glad with exceeding joy.

—1 PETER 4:12–13

The righteous cry out, and the LORD hears,
*   And delivers them out of all their troubles.*

—PSALM 34:17

CRISIS SCRIPTURE GUIDE
Weakness

And He said to me, "My grace is sufficient for you, for My strength is made perfect in weakness." Therefore most gladly I will rather boast in my infirmities, that the power of Christ may rest upon me.

—2 CORINTHIANS 12:9

"Come to Me, all you who labor and are heavy laden, and I will give you rest. Take My yoke upon you and learn from Me, for I am gentle and lowly in heart, and you will find rest for your souls. For My yoke is easy and My burden is light."

—MATTHEW 11:28–30

My help comes from the LORD,
Who made heaven and earth.
He will not allow your foot to be moved;
He who keeps you will not slumber.

—PSALM 121:2–3

Worldliness

"Now these are the ones sown among thorns; they are the ones who hear the word, and the cares of this world, the deceitfulness of riches, and the desires for other things entering in choke the word, and it becomes unfruitful. But these are the ones sown on good ground, those who hear the word, accept it, and bear fruit: some thirtyfold, some sixty, and some a hundred."

—MARK 4:18–20

Do not love the world or the things in the world. If anyone loves the world, the love of the Father is not in him. For all that is in the world—the lust of the flesh, the lust of the eyes, and the pride of life—is not of the Father but is of the world. And the world is passing away, and the lust of it; but he who does the will of God abides forever.

—1 JOHN 2:15–17

Notes

Notes

....
....
....
....
....
....
....
....
....
....
....
....
....
....
....
....
....

Notes

Notes